RIDING THE DRAGON

Roselle Angwin has spent twenty years studying and working with systems of psychological and spiritual transformation. She is particularly interested in personal mythology, and as a poet, flautist and craftswoman is fascinated by the relationship between the creative process and the unconscious. She has developed and run highly successful workshops on these themes.

Riding the Dragon

MYTH AND THE
INNER JOURNEY

Roselle Angwin

ELEMENT

Shaftesbury, Dorset ● Rockport, Massachusetts
Brisbane, Queensland

First published in Great Britain in 1994 by
Element Books Limited
Shaftesbury, Dorset

Published in the USA in 1994 by
Element, Inc.
42 Broadway, Rockport, MA 01966

Published in Australia in 1994 by
Element Books Limited for
Jacaranda Wiley Limited
33 Park Road, Milton, Brisbane, 4064

Cover illustration courtesy of Image Colour Library
Cover design by Max Fairbrother
Design by Roger Lightfoot
Typeset by Footnote Graphics, Warminster, Wiltshire
Printed and bound in Great Britain by
Redwood Books Ltd, Trowbridge, Wiltshire

British Library Cataloguing in Publication
data available

Library of Congress Cataloging in Publication
data available

ISBN 1–85230–575–4

Contents

Contents

This book is dedicated to Eloise, with my love. And to all those who know that the only path is the Path with Heart. May you always walk lightly on this earth.

Acknowledgements

My love and thanks are due to very many people, far more than I can list here.

Firstly my gratitude to the Edgar Cayce Foundation and the ARE Press for their kind permission to reprint several pages from Mark Thurston's book *Discovering Your Soul's Purpose* (ARE Press, 1984). In Chapter 2 I've included two poems from *Times Alone: Selected Poems of Antonio Machado* (Wesleyan University Press, 1983; translation copyright 1983 by Robert Bly, reprinted with his permission). My thanks to him, too, for this and for much inspiration. Here, too, I should mention the many authors and publishers of books that have been inspiring or helpful, or both, in the writing of this book, as well as in my own life. I have included some of these in the Notes section.

Warm thanks and love are due to Joan and Reyn Swallow, of the Transpersonal Psychology Study Centre, for 'lighting the touch-paper', and for much wisdom. This book has grown out of the work that I did with them. Thanks, too, to Ian Gordon-Brown (and Barbara Somers) of the Centre for Transpersonal Psychology for permission to use the 'Lighted Field of Consciousness' model. Also to my workshop participants for the feedback; notably Steve Tyrrell, who, as a writer himself, taught me the value of structure and form.

My parents, sisters, extended family and friends have been continuously loving and supportive. Eloise, my daughter, has been endlessly tolerant of an erratic lifestyle, a busy mother and little money, and has consistently offered love rather than the (quite legitimate) complaints that another person might have made. She has always been an enormous plus in my life. My friends deserve special thanks for love, support and nourishment in all forms, and for the frequency with which they have helped me pick up the pieces; in particular Sarah and David, Stuart and Alison, and Francis and Hanneke. Also Bridget, Si, Nic, Sarah V., Anne J., Judy, Annie P., Nicky H.,

Dave and Sandy and the Barnicoats, and my many other friends too numerous to mention. My love to you all.

I'd like also to thank JB, who accompanied me the first time to the Grail Castle, where I neglected to ask the question. And also and especially ABP, for the wings.

Acknowledgement too to my supposed ancestors, the Angevins. I discovered during the course of writing this book that the members of the House of Anjou were the legendary Keepers of the Grail.

Myth is the secret opening through which the inexhaustible energies of the cosmos pour into human cultural manifestation.

Joseph Campbell[1]

Prologue

In the beginning, before our earth was born, was the most mighty explosion, and streaming across space were sent billion upon billion of flaming fragments. At the heart of all matter still smoulders a tiny spark of the original star-fire, waiting for breath . . .

In our society at the end of the twentieth century, most of us spend so much time involved in the 'outer world' as our main reality that we overlook the riches of our inner world, to our own cost. 'Where there is no vision the people perish', and vision and wisdom require a willingness to look within.

There is, however, no matter how much we try to ignore or evade it, a deep need within the human psyche to change, grow and evolve, to move from feelings of isolation and limitation towards a sense of fulfilment, unity and connectedness with all life. Rather than simply seeking pleasure or happiness, at a more profound level we are seeking wholeness, integration, freedom, meaning. But we have collectively reached a stage where not only are our own individual souls but also the world-soul, *anima mundi*, under threat. The word soul itself has become diminished, outmoded, sentimentalized and literally denatured, and imagination and meaning are endangered species in a world that above all else values factual information, and the voracious devouring of anything unfortunate enough as to be labelled a 'resource'. It is left to the artists, poets, musicians, storytellers and visionaries – once at the heart of society, now seen as peripheral – to keep alight the torches of wisdom, inspiration, imagination.

We do, of course, have a choice. We can continue to ignore the inner voices, to run blindly from our own dark shadow, to see 'the enemy' out there. We can pretend that everything is all right and feed our inner emptiness with outer goodies. We can continue to keep our inner gods and goddesses, demons and angels in banishment, to remain blindly unconscious of what we are doing to ourselves and the world around us. But the old gods and goddesses of the inner pantheon have a way of making themselves felt, if left unhonoured too long – on an inner level as personal crises, on a collective level on a larger scale in the form of wars, social violence, revolutions, oppressive regimes and so on.

Or we can choose to take the other path, to listen to the inner voices, to look for ways of restoring soul to the world. In other words, if we go willingly into the secret places of our inner worlds, our unconscious, in a spirit of trust and open enquiry, we may find that what we had supposed to be dark and frightening is actually a treasure-house of riches (and besides, going willingly may help avert some of the thunderbolts that an unacknowledged unconscious tends to unleash in our outer lives!)

One way of making our entrance into the world of the unconscious is through the gateway of myth. Storytelling, as the novelist Lindsay Clarke remarks, opens a passage from feeling to meaning, converts raw matter to order.

Myths and legends, such as the story of the 'Quest for the Holy Grail', for instance, embody universal truths that can guide us towards transformation. Although they appear to depict outer historical or fictitious events, they are actually maps of inner spiritual or psychological journeys.

Myths speak powerfully to our subconscious minds, directly addressing the archetypes of our inner worlds in a symbolic language that bypasses our rational thought-processes and that fires our creative imagination. Myths are carriers of energy, ladders between the worlds. Because of their archetypal nature they also give us a bridge between the personal and the universal. Through myth our griefs and our joys are made both greater and smaller than they seem in individual isolation – smaller because myth gives us a wider perspective, and larger because we see them as part of the universal experience of the 'human condition'. Myth gives us a distance, too, that enables us to break free of our habitual ways of seeing and being and to explore the recurring patterns in our lives in a less threatening, because it is less personal, way.

So what we could call Personal Mythology work is about soul, about imagination, about opening the inner eyes, about bringing into the light of consciousness that which is unconscious. It is about restoring the language of symbol and meaning to a world that can at times seem increasingly arid, frighteningly violent, destructively blind. Simply to choose to live in a way that is as fully conscious as possible, that causes as little harm as possible as much of the time as possible, is a major step. The oracle at Delphi had one message – Know Thyself – and to embark on the path towards self-knowledge is to recognize that we create and recreate the world each moment, in the way that we live. This in itself is a positive contribution, and enormously empowering; and more – it may go some way towards blowing on the embers of our star-fire, lighting the way for others as well as ourselves.

Introduction and Author's Note

And so the fire grows low and smoulders,
In the flames strange beings dance;
We live our lives as we are born to –
Choice, to some; to others, chance.

Without going out of one's front door one can know the whole
world

Lao Tzu

This book is based on several assumptions. Some will already
be apparent from the Prologue, and others will become apparent as you read.

My first assumption is that there is no such thing as Absolute
Truth – or if there is, we do not seem to be party to it on this
planet – and therefore any attempt at approaching the mysteries of the universe, inner and outer, is just that, an attempt; one
of many paths that lead (hopefully) to a greater understanding
of what it means to be human, to be here on this beautiful,
fragile planet of ours whose very existence is an awe-inspiring
miracle, at this time in history. So I make no claims to absolute
truth. What I am offering is a suggestion, one that works for me
and has worked for some other people too. Only you can judge
if there is truth in it for you. (I must also say here that, since no
book is born out of a vacuum, this work is built on many other
people's work; I have attempted to blend the wisdom from
many related but separate paths, some well established and
others less well known. The main influence has been that of
Transpersonal Psychology and the teachings of Dr Jung. Any
errors, incongruities and contradictions are, however, entirely
my own work!)

Another major underlying assumption is that, certainly as
adults, we create our own reality, whether we are conscious of

xiv

it or not. Our world is a product of the thought-patterns we generate, and the way we live our lives is a direct reflection and outward expression of these patterns. If we are conscious of this, we feel we have choice. If we are not, if we feel we are helpless victims of life happening to us, then we feel powerless to make changes and direct our lives. As very young children, we may indeed be helpless to change what happens to us or how we experience this; part of the maturing process involves taking the reins of our lives into our own hands, and if necessary choosing change; none of us *has* to be a prisoner of the past. John C. Lilly, in his book *The Centre of the Cyclone*, says: 'What one believes to be true either is true or becomes true in one's mind . . . these limits are beliefs to be transcended.'

We know that most of us function for most of our lives on a very tiny percentage of our full consciousness. If during our lifetime we manage to increase even only fractionally the ratio of our own personal consciousness to unconsciousness, then we have lit a candle for the collective consciousness, for a society is only as good as its members. C. J. Jung made the comment that it is up to the individual (that is, the individuated person) to redeem the collective, and it would seem that we have reached a point in history where we can no longer afford to remain unconscious. I've written this book because I believe that until we can begin to identify and heal our own sickness and fragmentation (as well as learn to nourish what is good and life-supporting in us) then we cannot help heal the sickness and fragmentation in the outer world. This book then is offered as my own small candle, lit from the flame of many others.

Something, somewhere, is wrong. Many of us have a feeling that something is missing in our lives. Because our culture is outward-directed, the only place we know to look for what's missing is 'out there'. We are like the man in the Sufi story who was approached by a neighbour as he searched the ground under a street-lamp one night for a set of lost keys. When his neighbour asked him if he was sure that that was where he had lost them, he replied 'No, but this is where the light is.' In our frenzy to find happiness and fulfilment we run further and further from our Centre, the Self (as opposed to the ego), in a fruitless search for more and better to consume – whether that consumption is of material goods, or experiences, or even – metaphorically – of other people. Even our divinity, our God, in our culture is 'out there' – although for the majority of people orthodox religion no longer offers the answers they want. Surprisingly, though, religion in its true sense may offer part of the answer to what is missing, for 'religio' in its translation from the Latin means 'to connect' or 're-connect', and it is in part our sense of connectedness that we have lost: connectedness with our Selves, with each other, with the other beings with whom we share the planet, with the planet herself, with the vastness of this universe with which we share our starry origins.

But we have not found happiness. And worse, we have reached a point in our history where we can no longer afford to exploit our planet and its beings in the way that we have in the latter half of the twentieth century. Our collective future is more delicately balanced than at any other time in world history. The results of our greed, our over-reliance on resources and the refining or consuming of these resources are becoming apparent in symptoms such as environmental crises. Imbalances are becoming more obvious, perhaps most poignantly illustrated in humanitarian issues, where we stockpile huge mountains of surplus food, and, while people starve on the other side of the world, we spend our time in emotional detachedness discussing the political and economic implications of aid. We clear vast areas of rainforest in South America so that indigenous peoples become homeless and more and more species of flora and fauna face extinction, in order to run cattle to satisfy the Western demand for beefburgers. Some of us end up with exotic timber loo-seats or front doors and a few million tons of topsoil is lost due to erosion. The treeless tract contributes to an ever-growing hole in the ozone layer, and drought on the other side of the world, and frighteningly, we remain ignorant of our part in this. Violent crime and unemployment figures are both on the increase, as are teenage suicides. Stress-related diseases are among the major killers in our society. Industrial pollution appears to be here to stay. Our water is not clean to drink, our seas not clean to fish, our air not clean to breathe. Our immune system has been invaded; the immune systems of animals such as seals have been affected; tree diseases have become more widespread; the planet's immune system in the form of its protective ozone layer is no longer something we can count on. And this current generation has been born into a world that lives – for the first time in history – with the fact that nuclear annihilation is an actual possibility. A bleak picture.

And yet what is also emerging is that we are collectively moving towards a major shift. A time of crisis can be an empowering time, an enabling time, an opportunity to look at where we are and what we can learn. It is now no longer a new theory that a paradigm shift in consciousness is happening. It is a psychological truism that things tend to get worse before they get better – breakdown often precedes breakthrough into a new level. Human beings grow through self-discovery, and most people do not step onto this path until things become so painful that they do not have any other choice. Now we have to change, simply in order to carry on existing, and there are signs that the change is occurring on many different levels. Even politically, great symbolic events have occurred through the last few years with such leaps forward as the tearing down of the Berlin Wall, and the dissolution of our enmity with the USSR. These mark a watershed time where energies are in flux before cooling into a new form.

So there is hope. But despite the above, this is not a book about environmental and social responsibility – although these should of course be part of our lives – but about personal change, which is also about adding to the thin line of hope that still shines bright under the door of gloom. 'Better to light a candle than to curse the darkness', and my belief is that enough candles lit will help to tip the balance. Margaret Mead, the anthropologist, said: 'Never doubt that a small group of committed individuals can change the world; indeed, it's the only thing that ever has.'

I am not alone in believing that our current crisis is a crisis of meaning. We need to know that our lives are not 'pointless journeys through indifferent space but part of a larger more significant journey'.[1] Human beings need something to stand in awe of, and we are attempting to fill what is actually a soul-need with body-food (or mind-food or emotion-food), rather like pouring water into a petrol engine and expecting it to run, and just as crude. Psychology has offered some answers; but psychology alone is not enough. Matthew Fox has commented that too often we offer 'psychological cures for cosmological problems. What people are looking for is a big vision.'[2] This book does not promise answers – they will be different for each individual. And besides, sometimes it is enough just to know that there is a question that needs to be asked. In the Grail Quest, it was the asking of the question in itself that caused the waters to flow again, and restored health and fertility to the Wasteland. What I do offer is a map to a small corner of one of the inner domains, one that I know because I've been there, and a lamp to guide you if you decide that this is a path you would like to walk awhile; and the knowledge that you are not alone in walking it.

MYTH AS METAPHOR

Myth is a form of metaphor. It's the metaphor that's truly empowering for people. It allows us to see our ordinary lives from a different perspective, to get an intuitive sense of who we are and what is important to us ...

Jean Shinoda Bolen

Our work then as men and women is not only to free ourselves from family cages and collective mind sets, but to release transcendent beings from imprisonment and trance.

Robert Bly, *Iron John*

As I have noted above, most of us change only when we have to, when it becomes too painful to carry on repeating the same unsatisfactory patterns. As somebody once said, if you do what you've always done, then you will get what you've always got, which of course is fine as long as you are happy with the way your life is. But if you reach a point where you have to acknowledge that something in your life is not working for you, or alternatively when you know that something is calling you but you don't know what, then seize the moment – you may have stumbled through one of those magical doorways where anything may be possible, where the right action at the right time may bring about total transformation.

It took a major and enormously painful loss in my own life before I started seriously to question the beliefs and patterns in my life that were working against, rather than for, me. If we look at the world symbolically, archetypal imagery such as that found in myth can offer us tremendous insights into human experience. I can pinpoint the moment, about 5 years ago now, when I suddenly realized that not only was I trapped in a myth but also I was trapped in a myth with an unhappy ending. Out of that moment grew a series of workshops that I have been leading for the last 2 years or so, and out of these workshops grew this book.

What made my realization worse was the fact that I had to acknowledge that almost all of the other myths that attracted me strongly had tragic endings, and they were all tragic in the same way. They were all themes of loss and betrayal and (tragic) death. (It's more recently still that I've realized that many of the myths I knew, or at least the ones with which I was identifying, billed the women as the losers. There is, too, a wider picture; a reflection of the lost or damaged Feminine in our culture.) It slowly dawned on me that a lot of my emotional and psychic energy was being drained into these stories, which I was determinedly, if unconsciously, living out in my own life, with myself (of course) cast in the dubious but romantic role of tragic heroine. Not for me the moderate path of contentment – I'd rather die tragically in search of the distant peaks of Perfect Happiness than tread that path. The trouble was though that each time I hit another crisis, the distant peaks became harder and harder to approach.

It was still quite a while before, with help and insight from one of my very wise teachers, the realization dawned on me that I didn't have to live with either the myth or its ending (I should say here that the myth that had 'caught' me was the Celtic tale of Tristan and Iseult, a story I had known from childhood.) And in a wonderful example of the synchronicity of the universe, not long afterwards I 'happened' to hear for the first time an alternative version of the myth that I knew so well. It too was the story of Tristan and Iseult, greatly condensed, and it seemed to me slick and unsatisfying. But it had a resolution – there was difficulty, certainly, but no tragedy, no loss – *and it had a happy ending*! It all seemed a bit too cosy and comfortable for my liking, but something inside me raised its head and breathed a sigh of relief.

I have been literally rewriting my myth ever since. I'm not there yet, but I recognize the warning signs of a slip back into Tragic Heroine these days. I have also developed various strategies for countering the pull of a myth with an unhappy ending – these will be looked at in the course of this book. But – just in case you think I'm advocating the cosy and comfortable approach these days – I must warn you that myths with happy endings aren't necessarily any better for you – sorry! – not at least if, for instance, in order to get your prince you have to grub around in the ashes while everyone else gets to go to the ball, cram your feet into unsuitable and probably painful footwear, be the butt of everyone else's envy and hatred, be a good girl and be home by curfew so that you never let the prince see who you really are, and finally spend the rest of your life expecting him to make you happy!

As a result of the enormous changes I started to see in my own life once I recognized where I was trapped, the zeal of the convert impelled me into setting up workshops to show everyone else how this could work for them! However, life as always didn't cooperate neatly with my plan, and what had seemed the pivotal point of a whole workshop has actually become peripheral. There have certainly been other people for whom this idea of identifying and changing a central myth has been enormously empowering. As happened for me, some people have found that it has dramatically altered their lives. But to others, the ending of their myth was unimportant, and some other part of the journey needed elaborating or illuminating or simply traversing more consciously. For some people, just looking at the same myth in a different way effected the changes, and the ending turned out to be wholly appropriate after all. Learning the language of the inner journey helps. What if, for instance, Cinderella was seen to be doing heart work, soul work, cleaning up the hearth for the fire to burn brighter, being humble and wise enough to recognize a call from the psyche to descend to spend some time in the realm of soul, the Underworld?[3] What if she was bringing a Zen attentiveness to 'setting her house in order'? And if she recognized the hate and envy of others and let them pass her by without getting dragged into them, maintaining a clear Centre? And accepting the limitations of being human and needing to be home by midnight? And what if the mice-become-coachmen were 'familiars', totem animals, symbols of shamanic shapeshifting that would transport her into another reality, a different kingdom where anything was possible? And the prince her inner masculine aspect? And if all that scrubbing and cleaning and maintaining an open heart was crucial preparation for the final Inner Marriage?

So my view of the healing power of myth shifted and grew. But however, one way and another, this book, like the workshops, has ended up not being just about myth. There are many good books on myth written by great authorities but what this is intended to be is a kind of guidebook to some of the aspects of an inner journey. My sources are many and varied, and, as mentioned above, I have attempted a synthesis of several different psychological and spiritual traditions, including Transpersonal Psychology, Celtic and native American shamanism, Buddhism, alchemy and astrology, to name a few. I have drawn heavily on the work of C. G. Jung and Joseph Campbell, and as I am a great lover of the works of Robert Bly, Jean Shinoda Bolen and Robert Johnson their influence will no doubt emerge now and then. As I have been writing this book, Clarissa Pinkola Estes' book on myth, *Women Who Run with the Wolves*, has appeared in Britain; I strongly recommend it for anyone who wants to take this work further.

I have used myth/s when appropriate or relevant, more as a vehicle to pass through one of the gateways into the inner world than anything else, and also as a voice for the unconscious. An inner journey takes archetypal forms, and myths are invaluable as symbols to help us on our way. A word on the title; I have called this work *Riding The Dragon* for several reasons. One is because of the mythological connection with Merlin and Arthur and the Matter of Britain. Another is because the dragon is symbolically interchangeable with the serpent, and as a very ancient archetype represents wisdom and knowledge (despite the bad press that serpents and dragons often have in the fairy stories with which we are familiar – many of which have been strained through the filter of Christianity – where they tend to represent the old religion, and evil). And thirdly, the dragon, as a fearsome, fiery and wild beast, represents for me our wild and vital creative energy, which is too easily stamped out by social norms and expectations and our conformity with them, and by our own fears. (There is an important distinction between 'wild' meaning pure, vital and untamed, and 'wild' meaning savage. I use the term as Robert Bly does in his work on the Wild Man, and as Clarissa Pinkola Estes does in her work on the Wild Woman. Bly in his preface to *Iron John* says:

> The savage mode does great damage to soul, earth and humankind; we can say that though the savage man is wounded he prefers not to examine it. The Wild Man, who has examined his wound, resembles a Zen priest, a shaman, or a woodsman more than a savage.

I feel that one way out of the 'lives of quiet desperation' (Thoreau) in which so many of us exist is to reconnect with that vital energy, and then channel it into creative ways of living. So one of the aims of this book is to awaken the vital aspects of ourselves that have lain dormant, and then on the back of this released energy ride forward into freer more joyful living.

The path of self-understanding, the core of any wisdom tradition, is not just a goal in itself but a means to a different end. The value of any path must be measured according to whether it is a 'path with heart', whether it increases our ability to be open, to live as lovingly as possible, to reach out to all other beings with understanding and compassion. If our understanding remains at the level of intellect only, and our heart stays uninvolved, then the path becomes an end and not a means. (The mediaeval romancers had a drastic symbol for remedying this: beheading. Sometimes you cannot see with your heart until the eyes of your head have been closed.)

For this reason, this book is not intended to be an intellectual study that you read and put on one side. In order for the work to take effect it needs to be taken down into the depths and up into the heights of your being. Its power lies in your willingness to complete the exercises that appear at the end of most chapters. Just to read them through will change nothing. And don't be fooled by their apparent simplicity. If you follow the instructions given later and approach the work with seriousness of intent, you will experience them as quite profoundly transformative (a word of warning – they should not be treated as party-games, to be tried out on your friends – inner landscapes require the same kind of respect as outer foreign travel demands).

How To Use This Book

Like any other journey, preparation is vital. Chapter 1 will explore in greater depth how to approach this work, but a brief word here. The book is not intended as a substitute for a human guide – therapist, teacher, mentor or fellow traveller – and I would like to stress that responsibility for the use made of the journey outlined in these pages rests solely with the reader. Inner work, even when gentle, can stir up a lot of psychic mud, and inner change will generally bring in its wake some outer turbulence as you reassess and adjust, and there is often resistance to change in those close to you – even positive change can be perceived as very threatening. Dr Jung stated that increased consciousness brings increased responsibility, and in any work of this nature there will be times when you wish you had never started – just as there will be times when you can't imagine how you ever lived before. The peaks may be higher and the troughs lower, at least to start with. It may be worth considering whether you have somewhere to turn for emotional support when needed; a close friend whom you trust, a personal development group, maybe a therapist. If you have some experience of personal development work, or a regular spiritual practice, it will enhance this work, as well as enable you to handle the changes more easily. And it's only fair to warn you now that if you feel that you are in an emotionally distressed state or have a history of mental illness, working with this book may be inappropriate.

If you decide to follow this path, then while the journey is very much about walking your own path in your own way, some of the exercises will need a partner, to 'read' you through them. Perhaps two or three of you could agree to make all or part of the journey together, setting aside regular time. Failing that, you will need to read some of the exercises into a tape-recorder to play back to yourself. It might be an idea to complete the tape with music that you find relaxing or uplifting.

You will not be asked to give up personal control at any stage in this work. Much use is made of creative visualization (active imagination), but unlike the world of sleeping dreams, where you have little or no control over what happens, in conscious inner journeying you do have control, and choice over whether to continue or to stop. That's not to say that there won't be surprises or shocks at times. The inner world has its own rules. If something 'comes up' that you feel unable to deal with, stop; and if necessary *take it to someone who may be able to help*. I ought to say, too, that some people new to active imagination find it quite difficult to start with. However, it truly does become easier with practice.

And lastly, for those of you who have some discomfort around the idea of spending time with and for yourself, I believe that time spent in 'setting your inner house in order' is never wasted time, nor is it selfish or indulgent. The purpose behind it is to 'give back', so that no matter where you are or what you are doing, you can live a more creative, fruitful and compassionate life, and assist others to do the same. Perhaps this way we can each know that we have done what we can to leave our bit of the universe in a better state than when we found it, and enjoy doing it.

> May the longtime sun shine upon you
> all love surround you
> and the clear light within you
> guide your way on.
> Incredible String Band

PART ONE

The Territory – the Treasure-house of the Unconscious

Listen to the silence
be still and let your soul catch up.
  Bishop Bill Westwood, on Radio 4's 'Thought for Today'

1

Creating Sacred Space

Side-by-side with our world there exists another time, another space, another world; a separate reality with its own laws, its own hours, its own possibilities. It is no less powerful for being invisible to our everyday eyes, or intangible to our day-to-day senses. It is so close you can almost touch it, and so far away that it may take a lifetime to get there. Entry is possible but the way is guarded. The price is that you leave behind at the doorway your everyday self.

All space is, ultimately, sacred space. However, all cultures throughout history have set aside particular places, as well as particular times, apart from everyday concerns and everyday reality, to facilitate entry into altered states of consciousness. The state we first enter in this interior space is given different names according to the prevailing beliefs of the culture of the time. Some of these include meditation, contemplation, prayer, worship, cosmic consciousness, union with the divine, oneness and so forth. We could call it touching the stillness.

It is, of course, not crucial to set aside a particular place, a particular time. At other times in history, and still in some parts of the world, the divine, the sacred, has been given space simultaneously with 'mundane' reality. However, most of us in the West live our lives at such a speed and in such a way that stillness, a prerequisite of gaining entry into the divine – or of giving entry to the divine – has very little place in our daily lives. We are as a largely urban race dislocated from our origins, and alienated from our natural rhythms. Very few people have a real sense of the flow and flavour of the seasons and what they mean both actually and symbolically in the lives of all of us, in terms of sowing, growing, harvesting, resting. Technology means that there is no 'need' to be aware of the rising and setting times of the sun and the moon. A wealth of imported produce and our own high-tech food industry means that whether leeks, or apples, or eggs are 'in' or 'out' of season is an irrelevancy. And how many people have any idea of whether the tide on the nearest sea-coast is ebbing or flowing at a given time? And how many people care?

The point here is that our highly sophisticated culture has made it unnecessary for our lifestyle or our livelihood to be more than superficially influenced by the circling of the seasons or the changing of day into night and back again. What we see as enhanced freedom comes at quite a price. We are out of balance, polarized towards day, activity, productivity, achieving, doing. We neglect night, passivity, receptivity, rest, being. As a race of light-lovers we have left no place for the dark (of which more later). Day and its activities can extend as far into our twenty-four hours as we like, or as our bodies can take. As activity-addicts (and I include 'passive' entertainments such as the television and cinema, theatres, concerts as activities) we only stop being outwardly active, by which I mean stop our addiction to continual sensory input, when we fall into bed to sleep. The dark – the dark of night, the dark moon, the dark of winter – and the receptive stillness associated traditionally with this time is not valued in urban culture. So we need to re-learn how to make a place for both these things.

In this chapter I am concerned with creating the kind of still space necessary for transformation to occur. Sacred space, inner and outer, is in a way an alembic, an hermetically sealed container of highly charged energy in a state of potential rather than directed movement. ('Hermetic' from Hermes, otherwise known as Mercury: 'Hermes guides the forming of containers, the establishment of boundaried places, particularly those areas set aside for inward work.')[1] In this place, 'the still point of the turning world',[2] we have left the world of duality and moved to a world where there is balance and harmony, where Heaven and Earth are eternally joined.

Images of this kind of set-apart space abound in art and literature. Traditionally the structures used all have in common a sense of enclosure, of being physically detached from more mundane concerns, places of refuge and renewal, inspiration and wisdom. They vary from oak grove to cathedral, initiation chamber to hermitage, holy well to walled garden, sacred spring to Medicine Wheel, stone circle to Japanese rock-garden, cave to monastery. They are often, but not always, circular, and in their obvious Eternal Womb symbolism they represent the birth–death–rebirth process of initiation. In crossing over the threshold into this sacred or ritual space, we are signifying our willingness and our intention to leave behind the known, our everyday lives and our everyday selves, and our submission and surrender to the Void. We are committing ourselves to sitting with the stillness, sitting with emptiness, opening ourselves to the possibility of change and transformation. Carefully chosen and properly prepared ritual space will reflect back and increase our openness to that stillness and the world it opens onto.

Given that we don't all have access to a walled garden or cave, we can nonetheless create a still place in our home or nearby and a still place in ourselves, to which we can return at any time. At the end of this chapter will be found a visualization exercise to create an inner sanctuary. Most of the work in this book starts and finishes here, and it will be important for you to become familiar and comfortable with this place before moving on. It will be helpful to use the visualization, either in its entirety or eventually just the Sanctuary part itself, as part of a daily practice. It can of course also be used at any time of need.

A great deal of the material in this book is based on the idea of expanding our boundaries. Much of it involves working with the realm of the unconscious. Before we move on in the next chapter to the psychology and mythology underlying this work, I want to look at the practical aspects of preparing the ground with a view to opening ourselves to extended/expanded awareness – while at the same time knowing how to stay grounded, too, when necessary. You need to be able to create a space where inner and outer, upper and lower realms can meet and merge without your being blown away. 'Centring' is a necessary part of this work (Kenneth Meadows, in his book *The Medicine Way* defines the state of being centred thus: 'A state of calm receptivity and equilibrium in which the attention is no longer directed to meet the expectations other people have about yourself. It is a condition of being yourself.') Meditation and breathing exercises can help (see below).

The aim of all personal development work is to become both more fully human and more fully oneself, realizing as much as possible of one's potential. It is about fanning the spark at our centre into a flame. There is also a transpersonal element to it that involves an enlargement of one's sense of relatedness and connectedness, one's divinity.

Throughout each person's life, there will be times when, just for a split second, there is a sense that the 'veil between the worlds' has suddenly become very thin, or even disappeared altogether, one's sense of separateness and one's everyday concerns vanish, and time seems to stop. The world glimpsed through the veil has a numinously beautiful magical quality to it. This happens most easily at adolescence, although it is possible that the pre-verbal infant naturally experiences life in this way most of the time, until conditioning and the ageing process combine to screen much of this experience out. These moments in adolescence or adulthood are sometimes in response to a catalyst, sometimes apparently spontaneous. However transient, they are so powerful that people may spend much of the rest of their lives either searching, knowingly or unknowingly, for a repeat of this sensation, this indescribable sense of transcendence and freedom and oneness, or mourning its loss. Being fully human requires an acknowledgement of this transcendent realm, and it follows therefore that optimum health also includes what Abraham Maslow calls 'peak experience', those types of experiences that even if only for a moment seem to take us out of ourselves, beyond our narrow egoic concerns. The realm we enter is one of dreams and visions, and could be called the Otherworld. Whether this is a part of the personal or the collective unconscious or has intrinsic existence of its own beyond human realms altogether is unimportant here. What I am concerned with is looking at ways in which to create or re-create the kind of space where this experience may happen.

While transcendent experience is a crucial part of the condition of being fully human, unlike some of the more ascetic spiritual disciplines the path I am outlining here shares the essentially shamanic belief that the senses of the physical body are very much a part of this transcendent experience and should be valued as such. They do, after all, provide the vehicle. Maslow, in his book *The Farther Reaches of Human Nature*[3] says that studies show that the commonest catalysts for peak experience for most people are sex and music (especially classical) – the latter also often incorporating dance. I wouldn't presume to comment on your sex life! – and neither, in this book, do I make much use of classical music, but I would say that our culture, with its emphasis on economy, expediency and technology, has done much to hinder the appreciation of beauty, and encourage the atrophy of the senses. So we are looking at moving more fully out first of all into the five senses of the physical body, and then expanding beyond them, so that these senses, rather than marking the limits of our world, become stepping stones, gateways into a wider larger reality.

STEPS TOWARDS ESTABLISHING SACRED SPACE

The Importance of Daily Practice

Try and establish time for any or all of the following on a regular basis. If you don't already have a discipline that you follow, this may at first be difficult. The regularity of practice is initially more important than the length of time you spend at it; if you try and thrust yourself into a rigorous schedule immediately, you are likely to call up your 'internal rebel' who will sabotage your attempts, rather like going on a severe crash diet with its usual subsequent 'bingeing'! So take time out to meditate, walk, breathe or visualize, whichever enables you to touch the centre, but to start with, make it only a few minutes a day.

Keep a Dream Journal

Record in it also any 'journeys' you make with this work. Both myth and dream are direct lines to the unconscious. Your dreams can help you see very much more clearly what's actually going on for you. There are many good books on dream-work if you want to pursue this further, but even without knowing the first thing about interpretation, insights will appear as you 'fix' the symbols from your dreams in your conscious mind by writing them down or painting or drawing them *immediately* you wake up. You will also pick up 'long-distance' themes underpinning your life that you might otherwise miss. Your dreams and your myth-work will also cross-pollinate, greatly enhancing the benefits of both.

Symbols give up their meaning gradually. Do not expect an interpretation of either dream or myth imagery to leap to the forefront of your brain each time a symbol appears. Other than perhaps what might be called the 'surface' dreams that deal with undigested daily matters, no symbol from the unconscious is meaningless, and every symbol that stays with you is important to you. Remember, though, that the unconscious does not deal in rationalities; and also some bargaining with it may have to take place to encourage it to yield its treasures. Its comments on some aspects of your life may be profound and illuminating; they are just as likely to be obscure and oblique. The unconscious may be devious, and also has its own sense of humour.

It helps to set up a dialogue with either the symbol itself ('what are you trying to tell me?') or with the unconscious ('I don't understand your message. Can you put it another way?') Answers come in many different forms; a word or phrase fleetingly glimpsed or heard somewhere; an unexpected event; a 'mirror' in your material life; a flash of insight apparently out of nowhere, or, of course, in another dream. Learn to think laterally and live symbolically; look for connections. Is there a link between your dream of being in a car whose brakes fail, so that you run into a wall, and the scene at work the next day when you completely lost control of your temper with a colleague, who then stalked out and hasn't spoken to you since? And when I have my recurring dream of driving faster than I feel safe in the outside lane of the motorway, I know that yet again I am on the verge of taking on some extra job or responsibility in my life which will cause physical or emotional burnout, and that it is time for me to say no. And watch out for subtle wordplay. There is the story of the woman who had a recurring dream about 'champagne', which meant nothing to her as she didn't drink, until she suddenly realized that it actually meant 'sham pain', referring to some situation in her life that she could readily identify.

Before we leave dreams, one helpful way of looking at a symbol is to write it down or draw it, and then immediately and without thought free-associate – note down all the images that spring to mind in connection with it. One or two will have more weight than others for you. For instance, here's one of mine, where I dream of a marsh (see Figure 1):

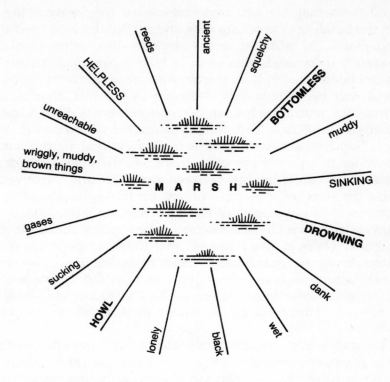

reeds
ancient
squelchy
HELPLESS
BOTTOMLESS
unreachable
muddy
wriggly, muddy,
brown things
M A R S H
SINKING
gases
DROWNING
sucking
dank
HOWL
lonely
black
wet

Figure 1

This says a lot about me! But the words/feelings that have the most impact for me are sinking, bottomless, drowning. Howl is also a strong one. Among other associations with these words is my memory of the horror I felt as a 5 year old at school when told that one of my classmates had disappeared in quicksand. So 'marsh' in a dream for me would prompt me to ask where in my life am I in fear of sinking/drowning?

Finding Your Power-spot

There are places in the landscape that hold power. These are equivalent to the energy-centres in the human body, the whirling vortices known as chakras, which correspond approximately to the glandular system. Both in the landscape and in the body it would appear that meridians of energy run between them. It would seem that our ancestors knew what they were doing, with the building of what are now ancient monuments sited at these places. In addition to the obvious sites, other places, apparently unmarked, also seem to hold a particular 'charge' that can be felt, not only by people who are sensitive to atmospheres, but by most people. Whether or not this 'charge' is intrinsically neutral, to human perception there is often a bias towards a 'good' or a 'bad' feeling associated with a particular place. Sometimes this is a collective or cultural perception, sometimes it is purely personal. It is more than likely that an exchange of subtle energy between perceiver and perceived affects the 'feel' of a place, building up further layers of reinforcement, a palimpsest of energy. Here we move into the realms of quantum physics, fascinating but outside the scope of this book. There is also a theory[4] that there are places in the landscape which, regardless of whether they are or not close to human factors, such as industrial pollution or radioactive leakage, are conductive *in themselves* to a high incidence of disease, or violence. These places, according to this theory, can be predicted.

Classically, high mountainous places are associated with yang, masculine, energy, active and outgoing, and valleys, especially river valleys, with yin energy, feminine, receptive and calm. So you would choose your spot accordingly, depending on whether you are wanting energizing inspiration or soothing quietness. The Chinese still make use of the natural energies inherent in a landscape in this way; their philosophy of Feng Shui is still in use when planning the site for buildings. Our equivalent, of course, is the network of ley-lines attested to by a multitude of authorities. Although these are not taken into consideration by our planning bodies, in a vestigial way subtle energy is still acknowledged in that many councils will still employ a dowser when all else fails – the nearest bureaucracy comes to acknowledging that technology doesn't have all the answers. Then there are the Songlines of the Dreamtime among the aboriginals.

So. No matter what you attribute it to, the fact remains that you will feel good in one place, and not in another, safe in one place and distinctly uneasy in a different spot. Spend some time with your intuition finely attuned until you find a spot in the landscape where you feel totally safe, and where you are unlikely to be disturbed. (By all means find yourself a stone-circle or neolithic burial-chamber if you want, but be warned, these ancient places channel huge amounts of energy that can be harmful to the uninitiated in a receptive and open state. Conversely, they can work to heal, but for regular meditative work I would suggest that you leave them alone.) Return to this spot as often as you can, and if and when possible, use this spot as your outdoor power-spot for the work in this book. Acquaint yourself with every detail and all the seasonal changes, get to know the trees and their names, the wildlife, the grasses, the stones, the mosses, which plants flower when, what time of day and from which tree which bird sings. Get to know how it feels at dawn, in the rain, sun, mist, twilight. Memorize the place so that you can visualize it when you are not there. If it's impossible for you to reach a place that is rural and unhumanized, then devote some time to closing your eyes and constructing in vivid detail your ideal outdoor place.

Reconnect with Your Senses

One of the characteristics of an urban culture is the under-development of the senses. Partly because they are no longer needed in quite the same way as they once were for survival, and partly because we tend to undervalue beauty and have lost the concept of the sacred residing in everything, much of the world perceived through our senses is lost to us. Out of habit we tend only to see or hear what we expect, and screen out the rest. We can expand the boundaries of our awareness thousand-fold merely by relearning the skills of truly seeing, hearing, smelling, touching and tasting things as they actually are. Human beings, unlike for instance single-celled animals, have a habit of editing sense-impressions to the brain; this means that 'only the simplest animals perceive the universe as it is' (Donald E. Carr).[5] Some censoring of course was developed as a survival-mechanism; it would be impossible for us to process the billions of stimuli coming our way every second without short-circuiting our brain.

How far can we un-edit, can we allow in the unexpected, can we make room for this world of ours in all its glory for our senses to roll around in? Playing comes into this sphere: when did you last dangle your bare feet in a stream, squidge mud through your fingers, roll down a mossy bank, stop whatever you were doing to spend 5 minutes listening, really listening, to a thrush's dusk song? When did you last fill up all your senses with the amazing miracle of a deciduous wood in April; the acid green of the new beech leaves against the violet haze of bluebells and the way the light shimmers and slides off the ivy leaves and the stars and flashes that break and re-form on a river under a slanting sun? Or the scent of moist earth after a shower, the stirring of a breeze in the crown of the trees and the mew of buzzards and the brief scuffle of a mouse in a bank, the feel of moss under bare feet and the rough texture of bark, the sharp tang of wood-sorrel leaves? Did you know that in the top inch of a square foot of forest soil can be found an average of 1356 living creatures?[6] Or that the roots of a tree stretch as far downwards as the branches upwards? What size universe can we let in? 'Beauty and grace are performed whether or not we will or sense them. The least we can do is try to be there.'[7]

Two more things should be mentioned before we leave this section. One is the importance of creative expression in our lives. It is all too easy for us to leave creativity to the 'experts', to be critical of our own unpractised skills. But to be able to leave our judgemental attitude to one side and to pick up a paintbrush or a pen or a flute for the sheer pleasure of painting or writing or playing, no matter how limited we think our talent is, is to open the wings of our soul. Try and find time – often – to work with clay or learn woodcarving or playing the drum; whatever loosens your being through the doors of your senses. Dancing is a great way into, and then back out beyond, both your senses and your emotions. Never mind 'I can't' – that's fear talking. Your body knows how. Dance to music, dance to the wind, dance to the sea, dance to your own voice-less rhythms. Dance your anger, dance your sadness, dance your joy. Dance for you.

And the last thing is to look for the gaps. A very useful exercise is to sit down with a pen and paper and an object to draw; a chair, for instance. But instead of drawing the chair, focus on and draw only the spaces made by the components of the chair. Look at the spaces in between the leaves of a tree, hear the spaces in between the notes of a piece of music, notice the spaces between people. This reversed perception 'cleans the windows' of our senses; and besides, the spaces in between objects are what enable us to differentiate between objects.

Celebrate

Make space for high days and holidays! Feast or fast, go to the sea, light a bonfire, plant a tree. Get together with family and friends, make music and dance – whatever makes you happy. There are always occasions to celebrate – birthdays, anniversaries, small and large achievements – but if you want further excuse, then remember the equinoxes and solstices, and the quarter-days (see Figure 2).

Ritual Space

Whether or not you have an outdoor power-spot, you will need to set aside somewhere indoors that you can use for meditational and visualization work. You will need an area with a space large enough to lie down in. It is crucial that it is a space that for a

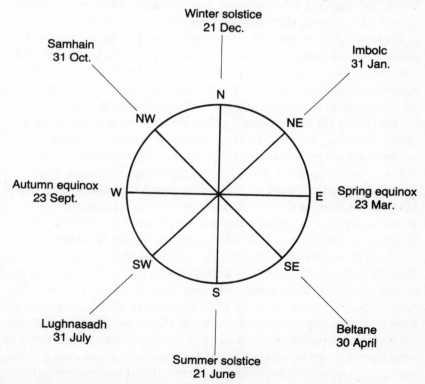

Note: Samhain, Imbolc, Beltane and Lughnasadh are the few great Celtic festivals. Each begins in the evening of the day shown above and includes the following day – the first day fo the festival month.

Figure 2

short space of time at least is completely free from interruption such as visitors and telephone. Ritual objects and gestures are quite important for the work. Joseph Campbell calls ritual an enactment of a myth, and *A Dictionary of Sacred Myth* by Tom Chetwynd says: 'Rites express the living experience of the collective Soul passed from generation to generation.' The Indo-European root of the word ritual means 'to fit together'. Ritual serves many purposes, three of which are as follows: it signifies intent; it focuses the conscious mind, thereby freeing the unconscious; and it serves to communicate by way of symbol or gesture with the unconscious and the superconscious mind. Symbolic systems such as the Tarot and the I Ching work on these principles, as do churches such as the Roman Catholic or the Russian and Greek Orthodox. Engaging the senses is generally an important part of this ritual.

Some suggestions for preparation for inner work are as follows. Do not eat immediately before meditation or visualization. If it is appropriate for you, fast for a few hours or longer if it seems right (although this doesn't apply to daily meditations.) A cleansing bath can be taken, perhaps with the addition of herbs or aromatic oils. In your ritual space you will need a candle and some incense or a burner and again some aromatic oils. Experiment with scents until you find the right one, or blend. Each oil has its own characteristic; some are uplifting, some relaxing, some inspiring, some soporific. A good herbal or aromatherapy book will help. You can use music if you like before meditating or working with visualization. I keep an object symbolic of each of the four elements to use in my ritual space; a feather for air, a shell for water (or a bowl of water), a stone or crystal or pine cone for earth, and the candle can of course represent fire. (The candle, too, is symbolic of the eternal flame of the spirit and of the spark of star-fire that I talked about in the Prologue. It acts also as a meditational aid for focusing the mind.) You could acknowledge the four directions with a few words at the same time as placing each of the four symbolic objects in its appropriate directional place. Making a Medicine Wheel with stones (see Chapter 4 for information on both) is another very good way of focusing your attention and freeing energy. It is also helpful to have a garment that you put on only for this work; a robe, a shirt, a cloak. Making or decorating it yourself will add power to it as a symbol. I also make a point of always keeping fresh flowers or a plant in the room I use.

During the Sanctuary visualization you will be given a talisman. This talisman should accompany you on all your inner journeys. It acts as your guide, friend, helper. Call it up in your mind's eye each time you prepare for a visualization. Its power will be enhanced if, after you know what your own particular talisman is, you make an image of it to keep in your ritual space – a drawing, a carving, a clay model – whatever is appropriate. If you find an appropriate object readymade, that will work as well. In a way the talisman acts as an Ariadne's Thread between the worlds.

'Closing down' after ritual work is as important as 'opening up'. Make sure that you allow time to come back into your body properly. Wriggle your toes and fingers, stretch, become aware of your physical surroundings. Ground yourself by eating or drinking. If you need to, use the 'Tree' exercise at the back of the book to earth yourself. Don't forget to record your journey in words or pictures immediately afterwards. And one last thing; let the symbolic content of your work unfold itself inside you before you talk about it to anyone else.

Breathing and Meditation

'Prayer is nothing but inhaling and exhaling the spirit of the universe.'

Hildegard of Bingen[8]

Breath sustains life. It is also a continual and unconscious mingling of inner and outer. The air we breathe is air shared with every other living being on this planet.

Breath can be used to create altered states of consciousness. The rhythm and depth of our breathing directly affects the pattern of our brainwaves. I'm not advocating here the use of extreme techniques of breath control, such as induced hyperventilation, or the type of breathing used to pass into deep trance. This kind of breath-work should only be undertaken by or in the presence of a highly skilled practitioner. Breathing can, however, be used consciously as an aid to meditative awareness by calming the body, stilling (focusing) the mind and heightening the perception.

A breathing rhythm that I find useful is a shamanic sequence: breathe in for three counts, hold for three counts, out for four counts, hold for four counts. Repeat for a few minutes. The speed of the counts is whatever is comfortable for you. You can use the same sequence slightly differently by imagining, as you breathe in, that you are inhaling particles of light that will flood through your body to fill every pore. As you hold your breath, see yourself glowing with light, and as you exhale let go of all the tiredness, greyness, anxiety and sadness that we all carry around so often with us.

There are a variety of approaches to meditation, and many different techniques. Common to most of them, though, is the purpose, which is to step outside the concerns and hubbub and distraction of that part of us that engages in the demands and challenges of daily living – our egoic personality – and make contact with that which is still and unchanging, whether we conceive of this as inner or outer. If we see our lives as a revolving wheel, whether we step off the wheel to the outside, or move from the periphery of the wheel to its still centre, we are acknowledging the Eternal in the midst of the transient. As we still our ceaseless inner chatter and tune in to what is real in us, so we open ourselves also to what is greater than us. Meditation, used skilfully, is wonderful for loosening boundaries and opening the heart.

Some people prefer to have a focal point, and if you are new to meditation, then this might be a good way to start. Set aside between 10 and 40 minutes daily, if possible at the same time each day, to simply sit and be. If you wish to use a focus, then choose a visual aid to concentrate on, such as a candle, or a verbal aid such as an affirmative or sacred phrase or mantra that you repeat over, or you could choose a topic to contemplate, such as love, or compassion. If you are sick, or troubled, you could use this time to visualize yourself well and whole and surrounded with light and love. Or you could choose to send loving and healing thoughts to a friend, or to a war-torn area of the world.

Preparatory meditation for the visualization exercises in this book however should include a period of at least a few minutes of 'unfocused' meditation. Whichever technique you use, the following ground-rules apply. Take yourself to your sacred space or your power-spot. Light a candle and incense if you like, and put on any garment you keep for this purpose. Remember that your body temperature will drop when you are at rest in this way – for both this and the exercises you might like to use a blanket. Meditation is normally undertaken sitting either on a chair or purpose-built stool or cushion. The aim is not to lose oneself but to find one's Self; not less awareness but heightened awareness and increased wakefulness. Nor are we talking about severing oneself from one's senses or one's ego; rather about expanding beyond the normal limitations of these aspects of ourselves. The wonderful Ngakpa Chogyam, meditation teacher extraordinaire, commented that in the midst of this free-floating consciousness you should be sufficiently mindful as to be able to answer unhesitatingly if anyone should happen to ask your shoe-size! Visualization work is slightly different. This is usually done lying down, where you will access more easily your unconscious mind. (Some people prefer to keep more control by sitting up for this, too, but the visualizations are then generally less effective. Be guided by your own intuition on this one.) Start any meditation with a few minutes of breathing as described above.

One approach to 'unfocused' meditation is as follows. As you breathe, let go of all your day-to-day thoughts and concerns. See the mind as a wide blue sky, stretching as far as you can see in every direction. Into this sky will sail the odd thought-cloud. Don't attach any importance to these clouds; pay no attention and let them drift by. Don't hang on to either the thought or the fact that you 'shouldn't' have thought it; rather just bring your attention back to the wide blue sky and your breath. At first it will seem incredibly difficult to empty your mind; we have so much unlearning to do. It truly does get easier, though, and you will come to look forward to this time. Just keep going, and don't beat yourself up when there are setbacks, as there are bound to be from time to time. Each time your mind wanders, bring your attention back to your breath. Be still, let go, and remember you are a divine being, lit with grace, and eternally connected to every other being in the universe.

Sanctuary Visualization

There are various ways of working with this exercise. The simplest is to read it through several times, until you have a clear memory of it. More effective perhaps though is to read it into a tape-recorder and play it back to yourself, or have someone read you through it. Take care to keep it reasonably slow, and the pauses should be 2 or 3 minutes long. There should hopefully be a tape available from the address in Appendix II by the time this goes to print, too. I should warn you that not everybody finds creative visualization, or active imagination, easy. If you are one of these people, don't despair – do the best you can, and it will happen with time and practice.

As always, set up your sacred space. Allow up to an hour of uninterrupted time. Prepare slowly, and spend a few minutes just sitting quietly first. Find a comfortable place to lie down, and cover yourself with your blanket, then close your eyes. When coming back out of the journey, bring yourself back into your body gently and consciously, and have something to eat if you need it. Don't forget to record your journey in words or pictures the minute you return to 'normal' consciousness.

EXERCISE: SANCTUARY VISUALIZATION

Imagine you are in a meadow. It is high summer. If you look around you, you will see buttercups and campions, swallows swooping, some poppies at the edges of the field, summer hedges, a butterfly or two. To your left is a stream; you can just hear it gently babbling. You can see irises and kingcups and dragonflies. Above you the sky is blue, with the odd tiny fleecy cloud. There's a light breeze touching the tips of the trees. You are alone, and completely safe.

Now in your imagination close your eyes, and notice the feel of the earth supporting your body, the warmth of the sun touching you. There is the smell of summer hedgerows – honeysuckle and meadowsweet. Still with your eyes closed, concentrate on your breathing for a few minutes. Breathe in to the count of three, hold for three, breathe out to a count of four and hold for four. As you breathe in, imagine yourself inhaling millions of tiny particles of light that fill your body and energize you. As you breathe out, let go of any tiredness or greyness or day-to-day anxieties. As you let go of each worry or problem see it floating off towards the stream to be carried away to where it can do no harm. Continue with this breathing for a few minutes. (*Pause*)

Now imagine yourself standing up and stretching. As you stand up you notice a path leading away in front of you, towards some woodland. Follow this path. (*Short pause*) Notice the scenery, what sort of woodland it is – coniferous or deciduous – what the undergrowth is like. Are there birds, and flowers?

Keep following this path. (*Pause*) In a minute you will come upon your sanctuary. It may be a glade, a hollow, an outcrop of rock, a hut or dwelling of some kind, a grassy spot by a spring, or a large tree that you will sit against or climb. Whatever it is, look at it carefully as you approach. This spot is known only to you and offers you refuge at any time you need it. There may be a being there to greet you, a wise person or animal or bird. If there is, take a moment to greet them and ask if they have a message or symbol for you. (*Pause*) Thank them and move on past to your sanctuary. Once there, sit or lie and be still. Here in your sanctuary is the most magical atmosphere of total peace and tranquillity. (*Pause*)

When you are ready, in your mind's eye prepare to leave your sanctuary. Before you leave, look around you – somewhere there will be a gift, a talisman, for you to bring back (unless you have already received one from the keeper of the doorway). Whatever appears is your gift, however surprising or apparently inappropriate. This talisman should always accompany you on journeys into the Otherworld. Thank the place and leave, taking the path back down. (*Pause*) You are now back in your meadow. Take a moment to come back into your body – feel the earth and the sun, wiggle your toes and fingers, stretch and yawn. When you are ready, come back into your familiar surroundings and open your eyes. Record your journey.

We are most afraid of the one thing we have come here to do,
and that is, to grow and become self-realized.
Agnes Whistling Elk, from *Starwoman* by Lynn V. Andrews

Very few people ever manage what nature manages without
effort and mostly without fail. We don't know who we are or
how to function, much less how to bloom.
Jeanette Winterson, *Written on the Body*

2

The Lighted Field of Consciousness and the Ocean of Dark Things

We do not become enlightened by imagining figures of light, but by making the darkness conscious.

C. G. Jung

In the preface to Gerald Jampolsky's book *Love Is Letting Go of Fear*, Hugh Prather writes: 'There must be another way to go through life besides being pulled through it kicking and screaming.' If this sounds familiar, then take heart – at least you are alive. If you weren't, you wouldn't be aware of the kicking and screaming! If you are alive enough to recognize the fact that you don't like this feeling, then you are alive enough as to change it.

I believe that human beings can change. Survival itself necessitates change; in fact, change is the only constant. Much of our unhappiness stems from the fact that we resist change; that we fight transience, that we want to fix life, our friends, our lovers, our children so that they stay right where we expect to find them. And in the attempt the fire goes out and we are left with a dead-feeling universe full of dead-feeling objects that we push around in a vain attempt at feeling that we are alive and in control. And somewhere, deep down, in a far-off place, a small voice tells us – if we allow ourselves to hear it – that there is more to life than this.

So one facet of the human dilemma is this. If we resist change, we are scared because life has a habit of rapidly slipping out of our control anyway and we are dragged along with it, kicking and screaming; if we don't resist change we are scared because we have agreed to dance with the unknown and by definition we don't know the steps, don't know the way, don't know the destination. But the difference between the two states of resisting change and accepting change is the difference between a death-dance and a life-dance. As anyone who has been through major emotional or physical trauma will know, resisting the pain only serves to increase it.

Paradoxically, the more we resist change in order to retain a sense of being in control, the more trapped we become, and what is truly liberating and empowering is to embrace the unknown wholeheartedly, to agree to 'learn the steps', to trust that some part of us knows what we are about and what we need, and then to jump into the abyss. You might as well go willingly – if you don't life has a habit of reaching up a hand and pulling you in anyway, one way or another.

I have learned much about how to approach the unpredictable by spending a lot of time around horses. Over the years I have ridden many highly strung and often young horses, and almost without exception I have found that if in my fear I have held tight on to the horse's head to try to prevent it bolting, rearing or panicking, I have made the situation much worse and ended up with – or more usually without – a keg of dynamite! What I do nowadays is to sit deep in the saddle, take a long breath, keep the reins loose-ish and go with it, following my intuition about using firm but gentle pressure rather than my fear about hanging on no matter what. If I fall off, at least I fall off in a more relaxed way!

At the point where we agree to sit deep and keep the reins loose, there is a breakthrough and we realize how much power of choice we have in the way our lives unfold. By recognizing how we trap and limit ourselves through our fears we can identify self-defeating behaviour and transform it into life-enhancing and self-supportive behaviour. We also free the people around us to do the same thing. At the same time we release creative potential to live our lives in a fuller way.

So one way in which we continue to allow ourselves to be dragged along kicking and screaming is by hanging on to our fears, especially our fear of change. Another way is to hang on to hopes and fears, desires and regrets, of the future and the past, rather than learning to live forever in each moment. And yet another way of trapping ourselves, and the one I want to look at in this chapter, is by identifying ourselves with our ego rather than with our essence, our true Self. This act pins us firmly onto the periphery of the catherine wheel, the carousel, or as I have noted earlier, splashing around in the concentric ripples on the circumference of the circle rather than sitting at the still centre.

Much of the aim of the first part of this book is to explore the movement from ego to Self, from peripheral living to centredness, from personality to essence. This kind of growth involves an expansion of consciousness as we become more familiar with our unconscious lives. The second part of the book looks at the part myth plays in this expansion, and the nourishment and creativity it can add to our lives. There are many maps of the psyche, many models of 'ordinary' and 'non-ordinary' reality. I have borrowed and adapted from many sources, but the underlying influence in much of the work that follows is attributable to Dr Jung, who has probably contributed more to an understanding of the human psyche than anyone else this century.

FROM EGO TO ESSENCE

Beyond living and dreaming
there is something more important:
waking up.
                Antonio Machado, trans. R. Bly

Mark Thurston, in his book *Discovering Your Soul's Purpose*[1] has this to say about the importance of contacting one's essential nature: 'Gurdjieff taught that one's destiny (that is, one's purpose in life) is contained within the realm of essence. Therefore to the extent that the essence is buried and subordinate to the personality, one's destiny cannot be recognized or lived.' So as long as you identify yourself with your ego, or conscious personality, only, you will be unclear as to your real purpose, that which will make your life meaningful.

So how do you know when you are living from the Self rather than from the ego? I'm sorry to say that you just do. Any attempt to convey it in words will fall short; rather like Zen, it is almost easier to define it by default, by what it's not, than by describing what it is. There is an absence of discord, of tension, of strife or striving, internal and external. There is no sense of 'I want' or 'I fear' or 'I hope'; in fact an absence of 'I' in general.

There is a sense of coming from the heart, a sense of rightness and reality about everything. There is an all-encompassing sense of compassion and understanding; a sense that everyone and everything is precious and magical and perfect. There is a sense of oneness and connectedness; there is no difference between perceiver and perceived; what you are doing for yourself you are doing for everyone and what you do for everyone you do for yourself. The most ordinary objects and actions become very special, each moment is imbued with a sense of peacefulness and fullness. Everything matters, and yet nothing matters. There is a sense in which you feel rooted to each moment and to the universe; not in the way our limpet-egos hang on for dear life waiting to be washed off our little rock with every wave, but in the way a tree is rooted; secure enough to be able to let go and dance with every breeze. Sounds transcendent? It is. We touch this realm when we let go to a 'peak experience' as described in Chapter 1. Most of us experience this realm when we fall in love. Some people, though not many, manage to spend a lot of their time in this realm – it can be learned, but it's a hard path to travel. It requires opening yourself time and time again to your fears, and to love. When you have touched the Self, living for any length of time just from the ego again feels like a distortion, a dislocation, a misalignment that requires psychic osteopathy. This is not to undermine the ego, however. The ego needs to be strong in order to weather the forces of transformation that are part of any spiritual path. But it also needs to learn when to let go. John Lilly calls that place where one may touch the Self:

> that rising quiet central low-pressure place in which one can learn to live eternally. Just outside this centre is the rotating storm of one's own ego, competing with other egos in a furious high-velocity circular dance. As one leaves centre, the roar of the rotating wind deafens one more and more as one joins this dance. . . . In the centre of the cyclone one is off the Wheel of Karma.[2]

In Figure 3 are two models used by Transpersonal Psychology to depict the essentially Jungian view of the relationship of ego to Self. They are pictorial representations of Jung's thought, devised by Ian Gordon-Brown and Barbara Somers and used with their kind permission. The first map applies to most human beings. The second model could be seen to be the

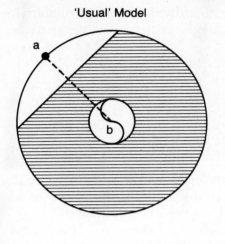

'Usual' Model

a = ego
b = Self
c = 'Lighted field of consciousness'
d = 'Ocean of Dark Things'

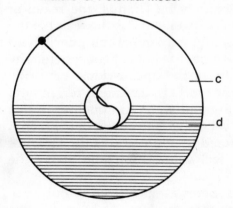

'Mature' or Potential Model

Figure 3

mature, evolved or potential model. You will see that in the mature model the Self has direct access to both the conscious and the unconscious hemispheres, and partakes equally of them. The connection between ego and Self is strong and clear. In the more usual first model, the Self is swamped by the waters of the unconscious, and the communication between ego and Self is intermittent and tenuous at best. As with all the models in this book, these maps represent a generalization – Ian Gordon-Brown commented that they break down in certain circumstances; they are not, for instance, applicable to the great redeemer figures such as Christ or Buddha, who would be unlikely to have issues relating to individual shadow-material, although they might still struggle with collective shadow issues.

A Map of the Psyche

> . . . without darkness nothing comes to birth
> As without light nothing flowers.
> May Sarton (Journal of a Solitude)

Various different traditions divide the world of the psyche in different ways. In order to keep it simple for the purposes of this chapter we will look at it in terms of three realms.

The middle realm is normal consciousness. The upper hemisphere is the world of the superconscious, generally regarded as masculine in quality, the realm of light, knowledge and inspiration, ruled astrologically by Uranus; the realm of Spirit. This world has a fiery airy quality and is the realm of the individual, the power of the one. A patriarchal culture will tend to value this realm at the expense of the lower hemisphere. The lower hemisphere is the realm of the unconscious, generally seen as feminine in quality, the world of darkness, receptivity, and instinctual wisdom, earthy and watery in quality. In this realm the emphasis is on the collective, the power of the many. This world astrologically is ruled by Pluto and is the realm of Soul. A matriarchal culture will value this realm above the Superconscious.

In the West the two hemispheres are polarized in our emotions culturally in a way that they tend not to be in Eastern philosophy. In the East, light and dark, day and night, male and female, spirit and soul are seen as complementary equals, each intrinsically crucial to the other's existence. The dynamic tension between these two poles is both the result of, and is responsible for, the continual cycle of the transformation of spirit into substance and back again. A third force – equilibrium – is born out of their union. This was recognized by earlier civilizations in Europe, too (for example, the Celts) but in our present culture, at least since the Age of Enlightenment (which of course says it all!) we are less comfortable with dark deep earthy feminine values than we are with the nice clean sharp values of the realm of Logos, although it seems that this is beginning to change at last.

No journey of exploration is complete without traversing both hemispheres. Both journeys have to be made – the journey to the upper world alone is likely to be 'ungrounded', to be short on concrete manifestation, and a journey to the underworld alone will lack vision and perspective. I have a theory, which is based more on an intuitive hunch coupled with observation than on factual evidence, that the upper and lower journeys are naturally made in opposite directions by men and women (I guess they then meet at the thresholds!) Archetypally speaking, I suspect that the natural journey for a man initially is up into the light, into the realm of individual achievement. His real tests and lessons come later, on the return journey through the collective hemisphere of the underworld. In order to achieve wholeness, a man needs to learn about relatedness. A woman on the other hand finds that her initial impetus, her natural impulse, takes her down into the collective realm first, and her real struggles and learning come on the upward journey. In order for her to achieve wholeness she needs to learn about the solitary journey of individuation. The word 'natural' is significant; but I suspect that the journey is influenced by the prevailing culture – that is, whether it is patriarchal or matriarchal (see Figure 4).

I should mention, too, a fourth realm as described by C. G. Jung, a deeper layer known as the collective unconscious. For the purposes of this book, I shall call this realm the Otherworld. Our gateway into it is through our unconscious world, possibly also our superconscious. The collective unconscious could be seen as a kind of metaphorical or psychic foetal sac and placenta, through which, with no effort on our part, we draw all the nourishment we need from the larger all-providing cosmos. If the personal unconscious is our individual repository of memories, dreams, hopes and fears, instincts etcetera, then the collective unconscious is the cultural store of archetypes, race memory and so forth. This realm too is the realm of the gods and the goddesses. It is this area which, through a direct link with the soul, provides a sense of meaning, mystery and awe in our lives. It nourishes, and is nourished by, creative acts. Our connection to it is kept alive by song, dance, storytelling, and by our link with our own instinctual and imaginative natures. It is wild and fearsome, and the more 'civilized' a person or a society is, the more tenuous the connection with this realm becomes. From this vast storehouse come, among

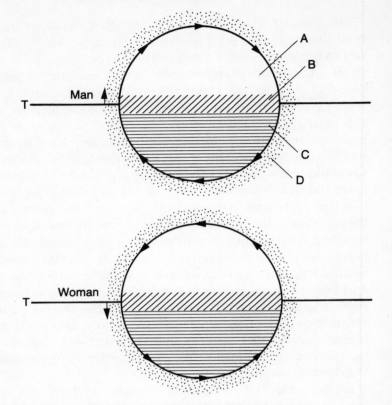

A = Superconscious. Light. Uranus. Spirit. Individual.
B = 'Day-to-Day' consciousness
C = Subconscious (unconscious). Dark. Pluto. Soul. Collective.
D = Collective unconscious (Other world)
T = Threshold

Figure 4

other things, our myths. If dreams are our individual myths, then myths are our collective dreams. A culture that (or an individual who) has become disconnected from this realm is in real danger of fragmentation, desiccation. Our psychic roots belong deep in this rich soil. Both Campbell and Hillman have suggested that a loss of myth in a culture leads inevitably to an increase in neuroticism, and James Hillman sees the process of reconnection as a vital step in 'soul-making'. This sense of disconnectedness from the deep unconscious runs right through a culture, so that 'because of our neglect the world is strewn with unrelated things' (Hillman).

The Shadow

> Look for your other half
> who walks along next to you
> and tends to be what you aren't.
> Antonio Machado, trans. R. Bly

A journey towards wholeness requires of necessity that at some stage we encounter, accept and integrate the dark side of our conscious personality, known as the Shadow in analytical psychology. In contrast to the ego, the Shadow is unconscious, and contains and embodies those aspects of ourselves that we don't know or we don't like, the repressed material that is not acceptable to the conscious mind – according to our own, our parents', or our culture's values. In our own time, the New Age movement has done much to increase awareness of a value-system based on love, trust and light, all of which are increasingly important in our age, but it is important that these things are not used to avoid embracing the darkness too – crucial for wholeness. Marie-Louise von Franz, who worked with Jung, (and made a lifetime's study out of the symbolic aspects of fairy tales), calls the Shadow 'the dark, unlit and repressed sides of the ego-complex'. Robert Bly, who has done much work with the aspect of the Shadow, says: 'The Shadow is the long bag we drag behind us, heavy with the parts of ourselves our parents or community didn't approve of.'[3] He makes the point that we spend our first 20 years stuffing shadow-material into the bag, and the rest of our lives trying to get it out again! By definition, of course, it is difficult for us to see our own Shadow, despite the fact that it follows close behind us wherever we go, and is perfectly clear to anyone else! (Sometimes it is a person of the opposite sex who helps us retrieve our Shadow. I remember as a child being intrigued in Peter Pan by the fact that Wendy re-attached Peter's Shadow to him. It is usually, however, someone of our own sex who introduces us to our Shadow.) We know when someone else has stepped on our Shadow by our over-reaction to them; the Shadow is projected 'out there', so that what we hate or fear most in another person, what makes us uncomfortable or angry, is a clue to what needs to be acknowledged and made conscious in our lives. The only way most of us can start to recognize and own the Shadow is by paying careful attention to our own negative feelings, to that which makes us most angry or hurt or uneasy or threatened or envious in another person. If we find ourselves using words like 'never' or 'always' to another person (you *never* do so-and-so; I'm *always* the one who has to . . .), or if we find ourselves critical of another person, there may be some Shadow work to do here. The Shadow is not always negative – it also contains our own unlived positive qualities, too, and much of our joy and creativity. Whoever is willing to turn and face their Shadow releases an enormous potential energy, an abundance of joy and spontaneity. In many ways the Shadow, being the unevolved, undeveloped side of our psyche, is rather like a frightened, clumsy and self-conscious three year old, and needs coaxing, loving and understanding.

The human Shadow begs the whole question of the nature of evil. The more violently we repress the negative aspects of ourselves, the more likely we are to project this negativity onto the outer world at large, onto our friends, neighbours, lovers, parents, society, or even whole races. When there is a mass cultural conspiracy to repress certain things, wars take place and genocide and holocaust become possible rather than unthinkable; the Shadow is not rational and we justify the most horrific atrocities in righteous indignation at the evil we imagine we see in the other party that of course *we* don't possess; it is so deeply buried that we have no access to it in ourselves. If we all took more responsibility for reclaiming our projections, owning our own darkness, there would, of course, be far more peace in the world. If we are sufficiently frightened of the dark sides of our nature to completely deny their existence, to lock them away with all possible channels of expression closed off, 'sooner or later there occurs a transfer of power, with the Shadow taking over total control of the personality'.[4] In this case, some kind of breakup or breakdown occurs, and psychosis becomes the only way of living out one's Shadow. The Shadow in a way represents a wound in the psyche, and to continue to deny it further reinforces the wound. Unless or until we are prepared to confront our Shadow, the wound cannot heal. It is only the exploration of our own dark side, and our wound itself, that has the power to heal us. And the bonus is that:

> whoever is not afraid to take this path through the darkness eventually turns into a bringer of healing, a redeemer. For this reason, every mythical hero desirous of becoming both healed and healer has had to come to grips with horrors, dragons, demons and even hell itself.[5]

Only the wounded healer who has healed him/herself can heal others. Astrologically, we could say that symbolically the time of the wounded healer has come, with our fairly recent 'discovery' of the planet Chiron, who represents this archetype.

To meet and embrace the Shadow brings new life. Again looked at through the lens of astrology, the Shadow can be represented by Saturn, the archetype of the great, wise and feared Dweller on the Threshold, who shines a light on our limitations, our fears and our weaknesses. A greatly maligned figure, he alone, however, can show us how to turn base metal into gold through an acknowledgement of our own hurting places, just as the oyster turns its pain and irritation (the foreign body in the shell) into the pearl – the Treasure Beyond All Price. (I connect Saturn with the Hermit in the Tarot pack who in solitude and isolation nonetheless keeps the light shining bright, guiding the way for anyone who cares to look.) When used correctly as a tool for understanding of self and others, the astrological birthchart is invaluable in its portrayal of which archetypal energies are at work where at the moment of birth. The esoteric thinking behind it is as above, so below; the planets represent archetypal forces inherent in both the macrocosm of the universe and the microcosm of the human psyche, and their position in the heavens in relation to each other is seen to represent differing qualities in the way that these universal energies manifest. So a birthchart, being an accurate map of the cosmological influences prevalent at the moment of your birth, can offer an insight into the way these influences or energies might manifest in the microcosm of your life as a human being. As a psychological blueprint it can highlight tendencies, gifts, weaknesses, areas of challenge, the style or spirit in which you live your life and so forth, and is a powerful vehicle for self-knowledge and transformation. What it does not do is 'make' you anything; your own free will is what determines what you make of your life. The placement of Saturn by sign, house and aspect is particularly illuminating; it can tell us much about the individual's primal wound, where and how it may manifest in his or her life, and what it needs for its healing. We will look more in Chapter 6 at this question of the wound, and its portrayal in myth and fairy tale.

We have not always been as afraid of the dark, of confronting our Shadow. One of our cultural taboos in the last century or so has been death, which we connect with the dark side of life. In our addiction to the light, we cut ourselves off, as I noted in the Introduction, from the natural rhythms of life, the waxing and waning, the time for doing and the time for being, the time of increase and the time of decrease. We accept the life aspect of the life–death–rebirth cycle of existence, but reject the death side, and thus also the possibility of new life to come. Our scientific sophistication disables many of us from accepting the symbolic mystery of resurrection, but we are caught between the rock and the hard place in that emotionally and existentially few people can face the fact that if there is no kind of continuation or resurrection we must simply just be wiped out with death. Caught in this dilemma, we just reject death and the darkness instead, and hug the light for all we are worth.

Fairy tale and myth, however, are much less equivocal. The Shadow, Saturn, the Beast, is purely the dark face of the handsome prince, as is the frog, and we all respond with a sigh of satisfaction when the heroine gathers all her courage and embraces the beast. It is not in the least surprising – in fairy tale – that he then turns into the handsome prince, marries her, and they live happily ever after. (The witch, the hag or the wicked stepmother represent the dark side of the feminine.) Something deep in our collective and individual psyches knows that this is just how it should be; the reward for courage.

Robert Bly mentions that in the Babylonian version of the story of the Flood, it is not the white dove, not the elegant swallow, but the black raven, the being from the underworld, who brings back the news of the recession of the waters. He it is who returns with mud on his feet. A clear message to embrace the darkness, the Shadow, as the bringer of new life; and not to be afraid of getting your feet dirty in the search! Love the clumsy, ugly, hurting, angry parts of yourself – they too need a little light – and unlike the more sophisticated conscious mind, they will display what they are with dazzling honesty, a true gift.

3

Fire, Air, Water and Earth – the Four Elements and the Four Functions

One of the wonderful paradoxes of being human is that we are all similar, and we are each unique. This, of course, applies to all living organisms, or at least the multicellular ones. The more evolved the species, the more differentiated the individual, and yet each of us shares common origins, characteristics and needs.

As far back as we can trace, it seems that humans have always had a need to make sense of themselves and the world around them, to classify, to make order out of chaos. While it is safe to say that we are unlikely ever to come up with absolute answers to the mysteries of existence, we will no doubt continue to collate, classify and interpret in an attempt to understand the secrets of the universe and our souls. We all do this to some extent or other; if we didn't attempt to make some sense of the stimuli we receive we would live in a state of permanent stasis. The way in which we do this, of course, in turn says quite a lot about our own classification or category!

While acknowledging that no one fits neatly into any pre-packaged category, some ways of understanding human nature are more helpful than others, and Jung's system of typology known as the Four Functions offers us a valuable tool (although opinion differs in the world of psychoanalytic thought as to the usefulness of its application in practice.)[1]

Jung suggested that personal attitudes show certain fundamental characteristics that permit us to assign them to clearly defined groups. In addition to the categorizations of introversion and extroversion, he noted four primary groupings that govern the way we relate to the world. These he defined as the

33

functions of thinking, feeling, sensation and intuition (Emma
Jung, *The Grail Legend:* 'The psychic functions are more or less
intermingled in an individual who is not as yet very conscious.
It is only with increasing consciousness that they become separate and differentiated', p.83). Sensation and intuition, while
diametrically opposed, are nonetheless opposite poles of the
same axis, that of perception. Crudely put, this axis enables us
to become aware of what is happening around us. The sensation pole receives information through the five sensory organs,
while intuition perceives by way of 'hunches', unconscious
contents and connections. This axis does not evaluate or interpret events, it merely receives what happens. The functions of
thinking and feeling constitute the two poles of the opposite
axis, the axis of judgement and evaluation. Jung says that
when we think it is in order to reach a conclusion, and when
we feel we are concerned with attaching a proper value to
something.[2] 'Sensation establishes what is actually given,
thinking enables us to recognize its meaning, feeling tells us its
value, and finally intuition points to the possibilities of the
whence and whither.'[3] (He also makes a point of distinguishing
between different uses of the word feeling (see Figure 5); in this

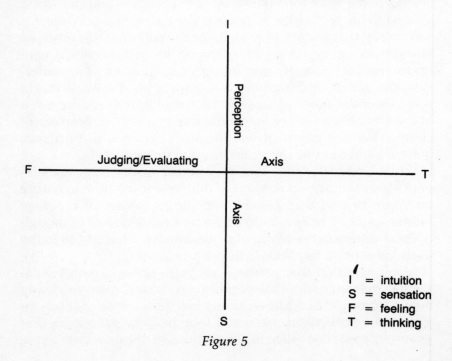

Figure 5

context it does *not* mean sensation-feeling, a tactile experience, nor feeling as in 'I have a feeling that it will rain on my day off'; but specifically as it relates to our emotional nature; feelings of regret, joy, fear, peace and so on.)

According to this theory, while all of us, of course, have access to all four functions, most of us will have one function highly developed, or differentiated, over and above the others. This pole represents the function to which we have immediate and automatic access. We are at ease, comfortable with, the qualities inherent in this function; it symbolizes our natural style, our everyday way-of-being in the world, our predominant way of relating to what is around us. Although access to this function is totally automatic, it is nonetheless our most 'conscious', because most developed, function. Naturally, the opposite pole of the same axis will be our least-developed function; deeply embedded in the unconscious, it represents the area of our struggles, the function over which we have the least control, and the one that when triggered by some event threatens to overwhelm us. We will look later at how this point of our greatest vulnerability can also become our teacher and healer. From a mythological point of view, we could look at the primary function as representing the king/queen (of the psyche), the two auxiliary functions (the other axis) as being the two eldest, worldly wise and talented sons/daughters, and the embedded, or 'inferior' function as the young naive third son/daughter, (sometimes represented as the fool), who nonetheless is the one who brings home the treasure – of which more later. The model of someone whose strongest function was, for instance, intuition, is shown in Figure 6.

This person would be an intuitive, probably highly creative and gifted, with much vision and warmth, and likely to have a mystical bent. He or she would be comfortable in the world of spirit, and would tend to move around by way of sudden hunches, happy to take risks and make instant changes. Life to an intuitive tends to be one long adventure (often to the dismay of the people who share their lives.) He or she would not find it easy to plan or follow schedules, would dislike being tied down, and would tend to be ungrounded; possibly idealistic in the extreme, with much vision and many ideas that would not necessarily be manifested in a concrete way (a sensation-function person might then pick these ideas up and give them a material form). The intuitive person's difficulties and challenges

Primary ('Superior') Function

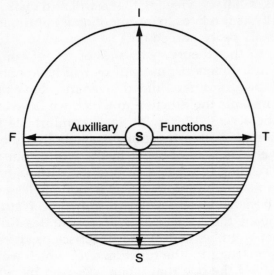

Embedded ('Inferior') Function

Figure 6

would lie largely in the area represented by the inferior
function, sensation, which would constantly threaten to overwhelm that person with material problems – money, cars,
structures, bills, timetables, health problems. The two auxiliary
functions in this case would be those of thinking and feeling,
which would give a sense of reasonably unobstructed access
to both ways of judging and evaluating the world; decisions
would be likely to be made from both head and heart in
tandem.

Some people, however, have more or less conscious access
to two functions rather than just one; their map might look like
Figure 7.

A person with this configuration would be a feeling–
intuitive, and these two functions together would tend to reinforce a general vagueness, idealism and 'unreality', giving
also a warm and outgoing nature that would be likely to be in
tune with hidden forces and other people's unspoken feelings
and moods. They would be likely to be erratic and 'ungrounded', and given to following impulses and wild geese. In
this case, both sensation and thinking, intellect, would be in

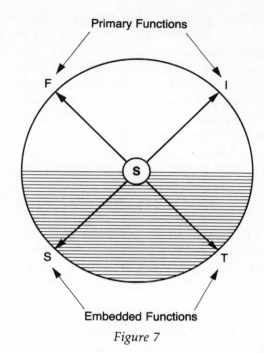

Primary Functions

Embedded Functions

Figure 7

the unconscious. If the picture were to be reversed, with sensation and thinking as the dominant functions and feeling and intuition buried in the unconscious, the person would tend to be a clear and rational pragmatic thinker, sceptical about what they would see as wishy-washy mysticism and naive idealism that could not be backed up with logical and scientifically viable proof. A person with this emphasis would be likely to be good at planning and organizing, quite possibly brilliant at research and analysis, dependable and reliable. They would be likely to be detached from their feelings and their intuitive nature, which nonetheless would hold a secret fascination for them at the same time as making them feel somewhat threatened. It is important here to mention that it is possible to be a 'feeling' type, and still be highly intelligent, just as someone who is a 'thinking' type can still be passionate and feel deeply. The different is in the mode with which we habitually feel most comfortable.

Just occasionally, something happens which Jung calls 'enantiodromia' (from Heraclitus; meaning to flow backwards). Something in a person's life, usually a major crisis, catalyses a sudden revolution through 180 degrees, and the function which up until now has been the conscious one is flipped into the unconscious, and the previously buried function comes uppermost. Needless to say, this creates much disorientation.

How do you discover which 'type' you are? At the end of this chapter will be found a questionnaire that will give a good indication. My gratitude here goes to the Edgar Cayce Foundation, who have given me permission to use this extract from the excellent book by Mark Thurston, *Discovering Your Soul's Purpose*. There is also a book called the *Myers–Briggs Type Indicator* that is an expanded version of Jung's typology work. There are workshops run around the country on the Myers–Briggs system, usually, I believe, under the auspices of the Quaker movement. We will look, too, at the symbolic systems that have the four types underlying them further on. For the moment I will quote Jung again before moving on to look at the functions and their connections with the four elements, both in psychological terms and in esoteric thought:

> Whether a function is differentiated or not may easily be recognized from its strength, stability, constancy, trustworthiness and service in adaptedness. But inferiority in a function is not so easily described or recognized. An essential criterion is its lack of self-sufficiency, and our resulting dependence on people and circumstances; furthermore its disposing us to moods and undue sensitivity, its untrustworthiness and vagueness, and its tendency to make us suggestible. We are always at a disadvantage in using the inferior function because we cannot direct it, being in fact even its victims.[4]

Ancient Greek philosophy was founded on the belief that all matter was composed of the four elements of fire, air, earth and water. This idea underpins much of both Eastern and Western tradition. Philosophies and systems of knowledge that make use of the symbolic concept of the four elements include yoga, acupuncture, polarity therapy, Tibetan Buddhism, alchemy, astrology and tarot, to name but a few. Some of these include a fifth element, which is most commonly seen as ether, or space, in which the other four manifest.

To the mediaevalists, these elements were primarily certain qualities inherent in all matter, and were basically thought of through their effects. They were based on the notions of hot, cold, dry and moist. The earth element, for instance, was the name for the combination of the cold and dry qualities of matter. Earth was seen as the heaviest and lowest element and had its natural place at the centre of the universe, of which it was the physical residue. Encircling earth was water, the cold and moist region. Outside water was the hot and moist region, the realm of air. Outside this again was the fire kingdom, the hot and dry realm, where meteors and other fiery ephemera were born (see Figure 8).

Each of these elements had their own 'humour', which had a physiological connection. In the human being, cold and dry earth was associated with melancholy (black bile). Chamber's Dictionary defines melancholy thus: surliness, dejection, pensiveness, indulgence in pleasing sadness. The corresponding elemental being for earth was the gnome. Cold and moist water was associated with phlegm, with its attributes of sluggishness, indifference, passivity, calmness. The elemental being of water is the undine, water-sprite. Air, the hot and moist element, governed the blood and its attribute was sanguine – ardent, confident, inclined to hopefulness (Chambers). Its elemental is the sylph, the air spirit. Fire, hot and dry, was associated with choler, the yellow bile. Chamber's defines the choleric nature

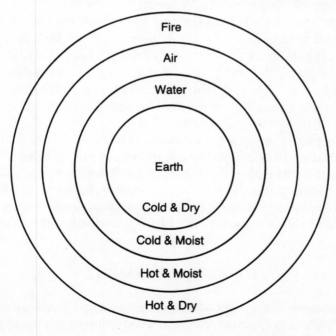

Figure 8

as bilious, angry, irascible, passionate. The salamander, a being which has a reputation for surviving fire, is the elemental for this quality.[5]

Each humour in its own way expresses itself passionately. Earth expresses its passions sensually, through the body, and its concern is personal. Water, whose concern is also personal, expresses through the emotions and sex. Air expresses its passion through ideas, communication, fantasies and causes and its concern is abstract but interpersonal. Fire's passions involve the creative process, vision, imagination and also crusades, and its bias is both abstract and transpersonal.

In order for things to be enduring, a perfect balance of the four elements was deemed necessary. Such transient phenomena as meteors, dew, frost and rainbows in this view are short-lived because the ratios of the elements each to the other are imbalanced. Diamonds and oak trees are more durable because the elements are in more balanced proportions; animals have shorter lives than humans because they are less well-balanced elementally than humans, containing more water and less air. In alchemical terms, gold, as the king of metals, is a mixture of all four elements in perfect proportion, and the same perfect proportion in the human body would give perfect health. The alchemist's task, then, was on one level the transformation of base metal into gold in the outer world, on another level the bringing into balance the humours of the physical body, and on the inner plane the meeting and marrying of opposites, and hand-in-hand with this the strengthening, tempering and transforming of his/her own inferior element, or function(s), to create psychological and spiritual balance.

The elements are in a simultaneous state of friction, flux and transmutation from one to the other. A potter makes use of this; clay is earth and water, hardened in air, baked in the fire of the kiln. A piece of pottery with time will crumble back into dust once more, completing the cycle. Each element, too, clearly has its own season and its own part in the birth–life–death–rebirth cycle.

THE EARTH ELEMENT

The *earth* element corresponds with the *sensation-function* people. People with this function/element predominant are most comfortable with the known, the status quo, what is perceived through the five physical senses. They are pragmatic and good at organizing and dealing with matter in all its forms. Sensualists, they enjoy the body and its appetites and strengths, and often are athletic 'outdoor' types. Many of them are drawn towards gardening, horticulture, building, and farming or working the land in some way. They often seem unshakeable, feet firmly on the ground, and offer solidity and support to those around them. They tend to arrive at conclusions by sifting factual information. Their qualities are solidity, security, substance, endurance, and they obtain much of their satisfaction in life through completing projects, tying up loose ends and finalizing detail.

Their negative attributes include stubbornness, rigidity, inertia, lack of imagination, resistance to change and new ideas (particularly if they are unproven or unscientific). Their eye for detail and fact does not always allow them to see the connections and meanings behind the facts. Their challenges and opportunities for growth will be most likely to come from the realm of their polar opposite, intuition; Trial by Fire.

(J. D. Smith: 'The trouble with keeping both feet firmly on the ground is that you can never take your pants off.'[6])

- The Tibetan Buddhist master Ngakpa Chogyam[7] says that the distorted manifestation of earth is Arrogance.
- Astrological correspondences are Taurus, Virgo and Capricorn.
- Earth governs the sense of smell.
- The tarot trump governed by earth is the Pentacle. The cardinal virtue ascribed to earth as described by a tarot card is Prudence (the Wheel of Fortune).
- In Celtic mythology, the four treasures of the Tuatha de Danaan each had an elemental correspondence. Of these, the Stone of Fal represents earth. In Grail Quest symbology the paten or dish is the image for earth.
- The earth polarity is female.
- Esoterically, the earth is represented by the rectangle. Its core motivation is to stay where it is.

THE WATER ELEMENT

The *water* element corresponds to the *feeling-function* people, who relate to the world via their emotions. Their response to a given situation is likely to be an emotional and subjective one rather than intellectual and objective. Their gift is empathy and they are often drawn to the caring professions. They are 'people' people; relationships generally mean a lot to them (with the possible exception of the 'loner' type of Scorpio). They are often dreamers and may be psychic. They lean towards being rather than doing. Their quality is fluidity, ripeness, smoothness, reflectiveness. The negative bias of water people includes moodiness, evasiveness, deviousness, clingy possessiveness, manipulation, martyrdom. They sometimes have problems converting feelings into words, and with articulacy in general – their challenges will tend to be in the areas of their lives to do with air/intellect. Their thinking may lack originality, opinions frequently having been borrowed from other people.

- Water's distorted manifestation is Anger (Ngakpa Chogyam).
- Astrological correspondences are Cancer, Scorpio and Pisces.
- Water governs the sense of taste.
- The tarot trump ruled by water is Cups. The cardinal virtue ascribed to water in the tarot major arcana is Temperance.
- The water symbol of the Tuatha de Danaan was the Cauldron of the Dagda, and in the Grail Quest the chalice, or cup.
- The water polarity is also female.
- Esoterically, the water symbol is a crescent moon on its back. Its core motivation is movement downwards, contraction.

THE AIR ELEMENT

The *air* element corresponds to *thinking-function* people, who are most comfortable when using their intellect. They are usually clear, logical, articulate ideas-people, often rational, reasonable and charming. They usually have a strong sense of justice, and freedom is important to them. Their airy quality gives them a lightness and mobility, a gentleness that is still often sharp-edged. They orientate themselves by relationship, and are usually sympathetic. Diplomacy and flexibility are often their hallmark, and abstract thought is second nature to them. More often than not, they will have a fairly clear moral philosophy, and their approach to life is based on humanitarian ideals.

Their negative manifestations include a degree of detachment from their own feelings, and therefore a denial or ignorance of other peoples'. They can be elusive, cool, detached and analytical. They have a tendency towards restlessness and fickleness, easily tiring of people and situations, endlessly searching, often discontented.

- The distorted manifestation of air is Paranoia.
- Astrological correspondences are Gemini, Libra and Aquarius.
- Air governs the sense of touch.
- The air element tarot trump is Swords. The major arcana cardinal virtue is Justice.
- The air symbol of the Tuatha de Danaan was the Sword of Nuada, and in the Grail Quest the sword again.
- Air's polarity is masculine.
- Esoterically its image is the sphere, and its impulse is to move to a different place from where it is, and to relate to someone or something else.

THE FIRE ELEMENT

The element of *fire* corresponds to the *intuitive* type. These people are creative, with vision, enthusiasm and passion. They tend to live in the world of potential, of future, and can be great innovators and leaders, with a gift for inspiring others. They embrace life, people and Great Causes with equal expansiveness and enthusiasm, and can melt even the most cynical heart with their *joie de vivre*. They are impulsive and dynamic, reckless adventurers who are happiest when they have a dragon to confront or a quest to undertake. They are often drawn to travel, and are usually in the vanguard of change.

Their problems come in coping with the world, and all the objects and people in it. Their negative manifestations include problems with commitment and responsibility, restlessness, impracticality, an inability to manage money – though they may be very good at making it, if they are able to use their need to gamble with life and their 'hunches' to speculate. Material reality has a continual habit of tripping them up, though, through the earth medium and its issues of health, security, housing, cars and jobs. Fire people can also be obsessive and destructive, devouring and consuming people and experiences in order to keep their flame alight. They have a tendency to get bored easily and to move on before completing what they've started. It is the excitement of beginnings that stimulates them.

- The distorted manifestation of fire is Grasping.
- The astrological correspondences are Aries, Leo and Sagittarius.
- Fire governs the sense of sight.
- The tarot trump associated with fire is Wands, and the virtue ascribed to fire in the major arcana is Fortitude (Strength).
- The fire treasure of the Tuatha de Danaan is the Spear of Lugh, and in the Grail Quest this corresponds with the spear or lance.
- The polarity of fire is masculine.
- Esoterically fire is represented by an equilateral triangle, with its apex pointing skywards. Fire wants to expand itself and therefore consume, and its preferred movement is upwards.

So *earth* issues are to do with substance, concrete reality, structures and order. Chaos is a threat. Earth is about making a place for oneself and one's family, about bringing into being. Also about physical health and fitness. *Earth tests* are tests on the physical level, and may be about how you handle money, or about your structures (house, job, car, family). They may involve an apparent breaking down of some or all of these forms, possibly illness (there may also be a reflection in your dreams at a time of earth-tests in symbols such as eating, digestion, excreta etcetera. Animals in dreams may also belong to this element, as representatives of the instinctual or physical nature.)

Water issues are emotional issues to do with belonging and connectedness, with deep-seated and/or blood-ties. They are about atmospheres, moods and under-the-surface passions (as opposed to the upfront passions of fire). The family and the collective are important water issues, and the intellectual voice of cool reason will be perceived as a threat. *Water tests* are tests on the emotional level, to do with feelings, relationships, crises to do with love, friendship, family; crises of introversion, isolation and alienation. Again there may be a reflection in one's dreaming life in dreams of water, floods, drowning or swimming.

Air issues are to do with communication, relationship, knowledge, ideas, language skills, harmony, reconciliation of opposites. Air, with the sword as its symbol, is also about learning discrimination, learning to discern false from true, real from unreal. Threats come in the form of highly charged emotional scenes. *Air tests* are usually about communication; there may be a sense of not being heard, or a sense that long-held beliefs and ideologies are no longer adequate. An air-test time may be a time when learning new skills is undertaken; perhaps a return to study. It may be that there is a depression that grips you to the extent that you feel unable to think clearly.

Fire issues are about meaning, creativity, vision, love, passion, exploration, leadership. Also that which is great and creative in the human race, and questions concerning who am I? What's it all about? Fire is threatened by what it perceives as too much order, deadening routine with no oxygen. *Fire tests* tend to be issues to do with meaning on a spiritual or intuitive level, to do with one's soul-path. A fire test often takes the form of a spiritual or existential crisis, when on leaves behind all that up until now has been comfortable and familiar; classic times of fire crises are adolescence ('I want to change the world') and again at mid-life ('I want to change my life') when important issues about how to live one's life come to the fore. These times may also involve a burning away of dross, a stripping down to the bare bones before new life can emerge.

A rough indication of which function is your predominant one can be gained from an astrological birth-chart, if you have one. The birth-chart is divided into twelve segments, or houses, in addition to the twelve signs. Traditionally, each house has a particular element ascribed to it (see Figure 9).

As mentioned above, each sign is also governed by a specific element. Counting up the distribution of the planets on your chart by element, firstly in the signs and secondly in the houses, should yield a higher total for one element than for the others. (The sign in which the ascendant falls is also significant, and if two elements tie for first place the position of the sun and the sign of the ascendant may be considered deciding factors.)

For a more accurate guide, try the Jungian Personality Inventory set out below. Obviously it is in your own best interests to complete it as honestly as you can, so that it reflects what you actually are rather than what you would like to be, or how you would like others to see you. As mentioned above, the inventory and the following guidelines are taken from *Discovering Your Soul's Purpose*; some of the items in the inventory have

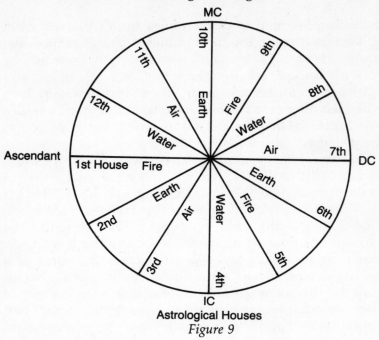

Astrological Houses
Figure 9

been adapted from the Gray-Wheelwright Jungian Type Survey and some from the Keirsey Temperament Sorter.

The inventory has fifty-four items, and for each you are asked to choose whether answer 'a' or 'b' best describes the way you are most of the time. Because it is not always easy to choose, there are five options. You can choose 'a' strongly or 'a' mildly, or 'b' strongly or 'b' mildly. The fifth option is to skip the item, if you find that you cannot choose or that both 'a' and 'b' are exactly equally true of you. Make all your answers on the answer sheet at the end of the inventory. *Note* that on the answer sheet the numbering of the questions proceeds horizontally. At the end of the inventory, after the answer sheet, you will find instructions for tabulating your results.

Remember that this questionnaire is related to your personality type – it is not a test of either intelligence or emotion. There are no correct or incorrect answers. Some or many of the items may be difficult to answer because different parts of you would answer in different ways. Try however to respond in terms of your most frequent and habitual personality. This is in distinction from how you would like to be, what you are trying to be, or what your current circumstances are forcing you to be. Also, the fewer items you skip, the more reliable the inventory.

EXERCISE: DETERMINING YOUR PSYCHOLOGICAL 'TYPE'

1. Assuming I try to be tactful, my more frequent impulse is to: (a) speak out, (b) be non-commital.
2. Assuming my financial needs were met, I would prefer to follow a vocation on the: (a) imaginative side, (b) practical side.
3. In making judgements I am more comfortable with: (a) logical judgements, (b) value judgements.
4. In general practice I am: (a) casual, (b) punctual.
5. Mostly I prefer people with: (a) good thinking, (b) good feeling.
6. When reading a book I: (a) often only read a portion of it, feeling I have got the main points and skip the rest, (b) almost always read a book all the way through.
7. It is easier for me to devote myself to: (a) social problems, (b) my friends' problems.
8. When I pick a gift for someone, I most often seek something: (a) I think will be a pleasant surprise, (b) I think he or she needs.
9. When my opinions vary from those in my circle, I am most often: (a) intrigued, (b) uncomfortable.
10. When getting ready to travel, I usually pack up: (a) at the last moment, (b) at leisure, in advance.
11. To me, tact is a matter of: (a) respecting independent views, (b) warm sympathy.
12. When it comes to making a decision, I am: (a) very frequently unable to decide because of equally attractive alternatives, (b) usually not hampered by equally attractive alternatives and can respond promptly.
13. Assuming I was equally familiar with both plays, I would prefer to go to the theatre to see: (a) Hamlet, (b) Romeo and Juliet.
14. If I eliminate for a moment my actual life circumstances, it is my natural impulse and tendency to be a: (a) spender, (b) saver.
15. Confronted with misfortunes for others, it is my more frequent impulse to: (a) search for the causes, (b) offer sympathy.
16. When it comes to practical life details, I tend to be: (a) impatient with them, (b) skilful and efficient.
17. When someone is talking to me I usually: (a) only halfway hear what they say because I am thinking of something else, (b) am a good and sympathetic listener.
18. Conclusions most often come to me by: (a) immediate inspiration, (b) practical considerations.

19. Toward goals once chosen I am: (a) tenacious, (b) readily reoriented.
20. Overall, people who know me best consider me to be: (a) full of high ideals that are often impractical, (b) pragmatic, entertaining only those ideals that are reasonably sure of being accomplished.
21. Assuming secrecy and confidentiality would be assured, my attitude toward a personal diary is: (a) they are a waste of time, (b) they are a valuable way of hanging onto memories.
22. When I find myself being neat and orderly it feels like: (a) a real achievement, (b) something inborn.
23. My tendency is to: (a) think more about the future than the past, (b) think more about the past than the future.
24. The way of coming to know something that has the clearest impact on me is: (a) generally my inner intuitions, (b) generally physical facts.
25. When I am around small children, my overall tendency is to be: (a) impatient with them, (b) patient with them.
26. I am tempted to new pursuits: (a) quite a bit, (b) only rarely.
27. When it comes to organizing things I: (a) am systematic and ordered, (b) prefer unstructured, flexible approaches.
28. When it comes to dealing with mechanical things or fixing things, I (a) usually don't feel competent, (b) find it comes naturally.
29. In general, the people who know me well would say that I am: (a) not a spontaneous person, (b) a spontaneous person.
30. I am a person who most often: (a) has trouble getting things done, meeting deadlines, etc., (b) is an expediter, a get-it-done person.
31. When facing a decision that will change my life significantly, I most often: (a) collect my thoughts and decide reasonably quickly, (b) am slow to decide and put it off.
32. When it comes to dealing with or discussing non-material things, I generally feel: (a) quite comfortable, (b) out of place.
33. I am: (a) not error-prone, (b) make a fair number of errors.
34. Overall I tend more often to: (a) see the big picture, (b) notice details.
35. When I think about the past, it is more often about: (a) the actions or happenings of events, (b) the feelings the events awakened in me.
36. When it comes to developing or reaping the fruits of my ideas and insights: (a) other people often reap the fruits instead of me, (b) I generally develop them or reap their fruits.
37. Without having looked at a clock recently I: (a) still usually know what time it is with good accuracy, (b) have trouble guessing accurately at the time.
38. My imaginings are: (a) of central importance to me, (b) curious and sometimes interesting to me, but not of central importance.

39. In trying to prove a point or get a point across, I: (a) am skilful in the use of words, (b) find that words get in my way.
40. My inspirations are most often focused on: (a) how things could be in the future, (b) how to deal with a practical life concern in the here and now.
41. When I have to change a pre-arranged schedule, I usually: (a) get frustrated or upset, (b) fairly gracefully adapt.
42. I am usually more: (a) speculative than realistic, (b) realistic than speculative.
43. Concerning the future, I am more comfortable with: (a) careful plans in place, (b) an attitude of going with the flow.
44. Living life with a sense of anticipation and of the approaching future is: (a) a good description of me, (b) not particularly true of me because I tend to live in an ever present now.
45. I am often seen by others as: (a) lacking enthusiasm or as being detached, (b) enthused and involved.
46. In my opinion it is worse to: (a) be in a rut, (b) have your head in the clouds.
47. I prefer experiences that awaken emotions: (a) only if they have positive emotion, or little or no risk of negative emotion, (b) any emotion (positive or negative) rather than experience with no emotional content.
48. I am known to people primarily for: (a) my ideas, my visions, the possibilities I propose, (b) my actions, what I have actually done.
49. I tend to be drawn more towards efforts to: (a) convince the 'head' of others, (b) touch the 'heart' of others.
50. I am more attracted to: (a) imaginative people, (b) sensible people.
51. Interpersonal relationships in my life are: (a) important, but not more important than some other aspects of my life, (b) clearly what is most important in my life.
52. I am more likely to trust my: (a) hunches, (b) experiences.
53. In judging or evaluating a situation I am more swayed by: (a) rules or principles than circumstances, (b) circumstances than rules or principles.
54. I generally view common sense as: (a) frequently questionable, (b) rarely questionable.

(Some items adapted from Gray-Wheelwright and from Keirsey Temperament Sorter.)

Having completed your inventory, you are now ready to tabulate your results. Your calculations will produce scores on four scales, one for each of the four functions of the psyche as described by Jung.

Riding the Dragon

Jungian Personality Inventory
Answer Sheet

	a	?	b
1	2		
5	1		
9		0	
13			1
17			2

Example:

choice 'a' is very true of me
choice 'a' is somewhat true of me
cannot decide OR right in the middle
choice 'b' is somewhat true of me
choice 'b' is very true of me

$\underline{4}$ (T1) + $\underline{2}$ (T2) = $\underline{6}$

$\underline{7}$ (F1) + $\underline{9}$ (F2) = $\underline{16}$

$\underline{12}$ (I1) + $\underline{10}$ (I2) = $\underline{22}$

$\underline{1}$ (S1) + $\underline{2}$ (S2) = $\underline{3}$

Figure 10

Work first with the vertical column on the extreme left-hand side of the answer sheet (see Figure 10). Add up the points you have assigned to choice 'a' for items 1,5,9,13,17, etc. Write this sum in the circle labelled T1. Then work with the vertical column of answers where you gave points to choice 'b' for items 1,5,9,13,17, etc. Write this sum in the circle labelled F1. Proceed in the same fashion in order to get sums you can write in each labelled circle (that is, I1,S1,T2, etc.) Finally add your T1 and T2 scores together to get your overall score on the 'thinking' function. Add your F1 and F2 scores together for your score on 'feeling'; I1 and I2 for 'intuition', and S1 and S2 for 'sensation'.

You should end up with a fairly clear picture of your predominant function. You will remember from the diagrams earlier in this chapter that some people have one predominant function, one undifferentiated function, and two that are more-or-less balanced, while others have two functions uppermost and the other two less differentiated. Very occasionally a person might end up with all four columns closely matched. If this happens to you, there are various possibilities; perhaps you are one of those miracle people so close to perfect balance that you must be virtually immortal! – or you were less than completely honest with your answers. It is possible that this inventory did not ask quite the right questions for you; it is also possible that you are at a crossroads, a transition time in your life. It might be worth running through this inventory again at a later date, or with someone who knows you well.

Before leaving this chapter I would like very briefly to look at ways of working with, stimulating, the undeveloped or 'inferior' function. This merits a whole chapter, but for the moment these suggestions will have to suffice.

If you scored low on *sensation/earth*: practice being practical, pragmatic, punctual. Consciously cultivate your senses and sensuality. You need to get back in touch with the physical body: walk, dance, roller-skate, exercise, go barefoot, learn the drum, make a compost heap, spend time around animals (learn to ride). Take up pottery, learn a physical skill: woodwork, mechanics, dry-stone-walling, thatching, basket-making.

If you scored low on *intuition/fire* make a point of indulging your creativity and your imaginative dreaming self. Learn to trust your hunches and follow your dreams. Value things that uplift and inspire: music, poetry, a sunset. Paint – especially with oranges, golds, reds, yellows. Perhaps you could take up hot-air ballooning. Have bonfires and barbecues. Lie in the sun (but don't forget your sunscreen!). Light candles. Take time off to daydream. Disrupt or forget your usual routines.

If you scored low on *thinking/air* you need to find things that will stimulate and sharpen your intellectual and analytical capacities; learning a new language, debating, writing, doing crosswords, logic. When you find yourself reacting emotionally, take a deep breath and try being rational instead. Learn how to plan, and practise making objective evaluations rather than personal opinions. Take up parachuting, hang-gliding or flying a kite, bird-watching. Go out in the wind, take a walk in a high place or by the sea and breathe deeply. Learn a wind instrument or a meditation technique that uses the breath.

If you scored low on *feelings/water* you need to awaken subjective impressions and focus on deepening or healing your relationships – with yourself as well as others. Get involved in the arts, and anything that will stimulate an emotional response. It may help to consciously exaggerate your emotional responses (you may need to warn family and friends!) If you feel angry, jump up and down and yell, if you feel sad, don't just cry, bawl. Get in touch with memories and your roots. Take lots of baths, swim, scuba-dive. Learn to surf or canoe. Take your shoes off and stand in a stream. Walk in the rain. Try a float-tank.

... nature is the matrix in which humans come to their self-awareness and their awareness of their power to transform.

Matthew Fox, Original Blessing

Man is fulfilled only when unseparated from his surroundings.

Lucien Stryk, co-editor of The Penguin Book of Zen Poetry

4

A Shamanic Map of the World

... a shaman is one who understands that life is in everything and that there are many ways of experiencing it. Being human is only one of them. A shaman is one who perceives that other life forms – an animal, a bird, a fish, an insect, a tree – experience life for what it is, and from their own particular perspectives. A shaman, therefore, treats everything with respect and learns to recognize the essential spirit of life in all things.

Kenneth Meadows, *Shamanic Experience*

NATURE AND THE SACRED

There was a time, before Christianity as we know it now, when humankind's view of the universe was not anthropocentric as it has been for the last few hundred years. The danger of course with a human-centred view of the universe is that a hierarchy is established that is dominated by the one(s) at the top of the pile; from this position it is inevitable that an 'us and them' attitude develops, and it is almost impossible to cultivate an approach to other beings based on equality, respect, sharing and compassion. Generally speaking, those at the top repress, oppress or suppress those below. Even the best possible scenario from this standpoint, that of stewardship, still tacitly assumes that we are responsible for the care and control of the other inhabitants of this planet. While undoubtedly we need to take responsibility for clearing up some or preferably all of the mess we have made of the earth, this is nonetheless the flip side of the same coin – it is our attitude that we know best and that we have the right to impose our 'knowledge' that causes the trouble in the first place.

If, conversely, we see all life as sacred, all life as sharing in

54

the divine, a different world-view becomes possible. Our care for the welfare of other beings comes then not from an attitude of dominion but from an attitude of the utmost respect, reverence and awe for the miracle of life and for the privilege of sharing this 'earthwalk', and a recognition that our common origins, affinities and needs require that we acknowledge the delicacies of our interdependence and our interactions; that we become aware that one small tug at our corner of the fabric of existence sends repercussive ripples through the whole structure.

The Celtic church and the early Christian church recognized the path of the nature-mystic as a valid spiritual path. (As far back as the book of Job (12:7) we find the following: 'But ask the beasts, and they will teach you; the birds of the air, and they will tell you; or the plants of the earth, and they will teach you; and the fish of the sea will declare to you.') The life of the early hermits, anchorites and anchoresses was extremely simple, and usually lived in or very near to nature, which provided the inspiration for much of their mystical and often rapturous experience. Tales abound of the early saints/sages and their common, yet to us almost miraculous, rapport with the animal kingdom. Since the late Middle Ages, though, as religion and science pulled farther apart, we as a race started to become estranged from nature. This alienation increased with the advent of the Industrial Revolution, and the gradual shift away from a rural to an urban focus. It is sad to think that in our age of increased leisure, increased wealth (we are told) and increased travel there are still children who have never seen a cow (let alone a fox), played with a dog, heard an owl or seen a free-range – living – chicken, nor even an expanse of sky and field unbroken by habitation, or a sunset over the sea. I suppose this applies to many adults, too. With the possible exception of visits to zoos or theme-parks, probably the only contact many people have with an animal is when they eat it.

Many mystics and thinkers have argued for a new religious (spiritual) paradigm that is basically panentheistic (as opposed to pantheistic) – that is, where divinity is recognized as inhabiting everything, and where everything inhabits the divine. Matthew Fox is foremost among these voices in the Christian tradition, with his doctrine of Original Blessing (as opposed to Original Sin).[1] He is the founder of Creation-Centred Spirituality, which has its roots in the Western Mystery Tradition. He has done much to restore love, compassion and respect for the earth and all her inhabitants in the Christian tradition, despite controversy and charges of heresy. (His position and the backlash it has catalysed is not new – Gnostic sects in the early Middle Ages were accused and persecuted for some of the same beliefs. The Cathars, or Albigensians, who formed a strong movement in Southern France and Northern Italy in the twelfth and thirteenth centuries, believed, contrary to the faith of the Catholic church of their time, that animals had souls, and it would seem that they also adopted a vegetarian way of life for moral and spiritual reasons. They also, incidentally, espoused the idea of reincarnation, and also assumed that women were as capable of performing priestly duties as men. They were massacred for these beliefs.)

THE PATH OF THE SHAMAN

So if every living being is seen as hosting a divine spark, every living being (and some would say also those which we call inanimate) is worthy of the utmost respect as our equal and our teacher.

This pantheistic attitude is also the way of the shaman. This is a celebratory path in which mutual respect, harmony and co-operation are integral values. Everything is seen as interconnected and interdependent. There is a strong tradition in shamanic societies that only what is needed is taken, and is replaced by a gift in one form or another. The energy or spirit resident in all beings is acknowledged as clearly as the form it takes. In this tradition, there is no conflict between energy and matter, spirit and body. The shaman travels with ease both in the world of everyday 'normal' reality and in the non-ordinary realm of the Otherworld. To the shaman, all things are sacred, and he or she 'sees no need for setting apart one day in seven as a holy day, since to him all days are God's'.[2]

The shamanic path is one of transformation, self-empowerment and healing. According to Michael Harner, the American anthropologist and author of the seminal book *The Way of the Shaman*, the word 'shaman' comes from the language of the Tungus people of Siberia. One way of translating it is 'to work with heat and fire'. If we apply this concept to a person, we could say that they work with energy to effect transformation.

A shaman is one who works with both outer and inner realities, changing consciousness – and even form – as appropriate, and walking between the physical and spiritual worlds as necessary to obtain help, guidance, insight, knowledge and healing for himself, another or the community. Gabrielle Roth in her book *Maps to Ecstasy*[3] puts it well:

> ... a shaman is a spirit worker. ... When people ask me what sort of healing I do, I tell them: If you've broken your leg, go see a doctor. But if you're living in your head split off from your body, if your feelings are choked up, if your mind is good at everything except what really matters, if you've lost your soul, if your life lacks spirit, then seek out a shaman. Or better yet, discover your shamanic powers within.

Shamans are the keepers of an exceptional body of ancient wisdom and techniques for healing and empowerment. Shamanism, says Michael Harner, 'represents the most widespread and ancient methodological system of mind–body healing known to humanity'.[4] It would seem, from archaeological and ethnological evidence, that shamanic techniques have been around for at least 20,000 or 30,000 years. Although shamanism has been passed down through thousands of years and many generations in an unbroken chain only in so-called primitive cultures which have not been completely wiped out by 'first-world' values, there is evidence that shamanism existed in a very similar form until the Renaissance in Western Europe, too, until exterminated, or sent underground, by the witch-hunts of the Middle Ages. It also seems that shamanic methods the world over share remarkable similarities.

Shamanism is undergoing a large-scale revival of interest. Much of it is in the form of Native American teachings, many of which are being released by the present tribal keepers of the knowledge for the first time to non-native people en masse. This has been a two-way process; more and more people are seeking to learn from these and related methods, at the same time as the tribal elders are in agreement that not only is the time right for this wisdom to be made more public but also that it is now crucial for the earth and the future of its inhabitants that we learn a different way to live. Michael Harner attributes this revival to various different factors, among them the need for spiritual and/or ecstatic experience, which contemporary shamanism provides without the need for mind-altering drugs.

Classic shamanic methods can also be learned and experienced quite quickly, inducing changes in consciousness that might otherwise take years of dedicated meditation, fasting and discipline.

Another reason that he cites is the increasing interest in holistic approaches to sickness and health, along with an increasing disillusionment with allopathic medical attitudes. Current holistic approaches employ methods that have long been used in shamanic practice; for example, relaxation and breathing techniques, visualization, consciousness-changes with their measurable alterations in brain-wave patterns, positive thinking, and drawing on sources of power that cannot be explained in terms of day-to-day reality.

A third reason noted by Harner is that shamanism offers spiritual ecology at a time of environmental crisis. He says that reverence for, and communication with, the other beings of the Earth, and for and with the Planet itself 'is not simple Nature worship, but a two-way spiritual communication that resurrects the lost connections our human ancestors had with the awesome spiritual power and beauty of our garden Earth'. He says that Mircea Eliade points out that shamans are the last humans able to talk with the animals. Harner adds: 'they are the last ones able to talk with all of nature, including the plants, the streams, the air and the rocks. Our ancient hunting and gathering ancestors recognized that their environment held the power of life and death over them, and considered such communication essential for their survival.' Whether we believe that such communication is possible is not as important as whether we are able to adopt an attitude that is both humble and open enough to recognize the importance of paying reverent attention to non-human life, and to our part in the two-way process.

Nicki Scully, author of the book *The Golden Cauldron: Shamanic Journeys on the Path of Wisdom*,[5] sees shamanic work also as a kind of mirror, where we work with nature 'in order to deify the qualities and aspects of ourselves that we need to consider and learn about'. She goes on to say that 'the idea of all the work with the different totems, whether animal, plant, mineral or the deities of various pantheons, is to have direct experience through our interactions with these beings that affect us in some way – physically, mentally, emotionally – and cause us to move forward'. If we look at shamanic work from a psychological or mythological viewpoint, the beings we meet represent archetypal forces, and as such each has its own characteristics, from which we can learn much about our way forward, and about healing the inner wounds and imbalances. We will look at some of these beings and what they may symbolize in Chapter 5.

Less well known as yet than the American Indian shamanic tradition is our own native Celtic shamanism. It may be more appropriate for British people to work with this tradition; partly because as race-memory it pulses in our blood, whether we are aware of it or not, and partly because most of us will find that the beings we encounter, animal and otherwise, in our journeys to the Otherworld are ones that we are already familiar with, either because we already know them 'in the flesh', or because they are embedded deep in our native ecological or mythological heritage. For instance, while most of us will never have seen a wolf, an eagle or a dragon, we can conjure up a mental image of them, and feel an emotional response. But 'coyote', for instance, to the average British person evokes little.

The bards and druids of the Celts were shamans. Apart from being men of wisdom, visions and healing, they were also known, as in any shamanic tradition, for their shape-shifting abilities. A shaman will have one, or many, power-animals, which act as guardian spirits as well as aids to entering and finding one's way around the Otherworld. The shaman, while 'journeying', will take on the qualities and perceptions of his or her particular power-animal, so being able to 'see' in a different way. A power-animal is also known as a 'familiar'. Broadly speaking, it is safe to assume that an animal that you have met four times, or seen in four different places or from four different angles while on a journey to the Otherworld, either consciously undertaken or in dream, is a power-animal for you. Michael Harner suggests that power-animals are always wild animals; my experience is that this is often, but not always, so. What you are contacting is the essential nature of an animal, and while it might be a little worrying to discover that your power-animal is a lame sheep or a battery hen, Celtic shamanic animals include the horse and the dog, both in my own experience and according to the comprehensive book by John Matthews, *The Celtic Shaman*.[6] (These two animals also occur in the Medicine Cards, based on North American Indian teachings, by Jamie Sams and David Carson.)

Chief among shamans in our culture was the bard, Taliesin. His story is appended to the main text of Lady Charlotte Guest's translation of The Mabinogion, and a collection of his writings form John Matthews wonderful book *The Song of Taliesin – Stories and Poems from the Books of Broceliande* (beautifully illustrated by Stuart Littlejohn).[7] Taliesin's story is a clear example both of shape-shifting, and of a journey of initiation, and what is especially striking is his movement, in the traditional order, through the four elements. In brief, this is the story. Gwion Bach, servant to the Old One, had among his tasks responsibility for stirring the cauldron (archetypally, the Old One is Ceridwen, fertility goddess, and the cauldron is the cauldron of wisdom, inspiration, madness and rebirth). One day as he stirs, three drops of the scalding magical brew splash his finger, which he puts to his mouth, upon which he is plunged into vision. He foresees instantly Ceridwen's huge wrath at what has happened, as apart from these three drops the rest of the brew is poisonous, and Ceridwen had been brewing the potion for a year to produce these three drops, destined for her rather backward son. He flees, and Ceridwen comes after him. He changes himself into a hare, and runs faster. She changes herself into a hound and gives chase, gaining on him. He runs towards a river, and becomes a fish, but she becomes an otter and dives in. He takes to the air as a bird, and she becomes a hawk, and just as she is about to stoop upon him, he sees a pile of grain on the floor of a barn, and changes himself into a grain of sun-ripened wheat, whereupon she becomes a hen and swallows him. Nine months later, he is reborn as Taliesin (he of the radiant brow).

THE WHEEL OF THE FOUR DIRECTIONS

Elemental correspondences figure strongly in Native American, or Medicine Wheel teachings, too, especially with regard to the four directions. There are different schools of thought on which element corresponds to which direction, however. Each system is, of course, valid, and an individual must choose the set of correspondences that feels right to him or her. I have worked with several different placings, and have ended up using the map in Figure 11, which I came across first in the books of Lynn Andrews, apprentice to Agnes Whistling Elk.

(As happened with Carlos Casteneda, there has been some doubt cast on the authenticity of Lynn Andrews' work, which purports to be a true record of her shamanic apprenticeship. Her books, however, are powerful and moving, and, whether or not they are 'true' does not invalidate the fact that much of their content is extremely valuable.) Although this does not agree with the more commonly taught directional system, and although I am not totally happy with fire in the north, the rest of the placement feels right to me. Perhaps this is a 'woman's wheel'. This system places earth, substance/matter/body, in the south. This is the placing of abundance, fertility, of love and trust and innocence. Things green up and ripen to fruition in the south. The opposite pole of this axis is fire, spirit and energy, wisdom and inspiration, the white fire of intuition and the originating spark, in the north. In the east is air, bringer of illumination and clarity, the discriminating mind or intellect. There is a trickster quality to this direction, something of illusion. Opposite air is water, in the west, the place of the emotions, introspection, change and transition as well as death and trans-formation.

Zoila, one of Lynn Andrews' teachers in her book *Star Woman*,[8] makes some profoundly perceptive comments on Western malaise. She suggests that the north element is largely missing in our relationships with ourselves and with each other. She says that men tend to live in the east, their heads, and women tend to live in the west, their feelings, and their encounters will be in the south, place of manifestation, sub-stance, where they might make love, make babies, make homes, sort out jobs and practical details, and return to the east and west to talk about their thoughts and feelings. West-ern thought and even Western therapy, she suggests, promote east–west movement on the Wheel, which certainly helps understanding and knowledge, with forays into the south to meet physical needs. But for a relationship to stay alive – whether it's with one's partner or oneself – there must be a dynamic movement north–south. This is where exchanges of spirit, of energy, of sexuality and instincts, of wildness, of the creative impulse and its manifestation, take place, and without this dynamic people and relationships wither and die from the inside out. So we owe it to ourselves and each other to find some way of contacting this spark, this fire, from the north, and to keep momentum in our lives by finding a way to express,

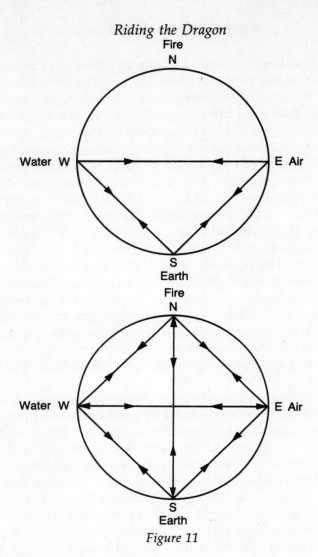

Figure 11

share and manifest our creative and intuitive impulses, those
things that truly nourish us.

MAKING A MEDICINE WHEEL

Making a Medicine Wheel out of stones is quite a good meditational approach to creating sacred space. Kenneth Meadows
says of the Medicine Wheel: '... [it] is a physical, mental,
emotional and spiritual device that enables its users to attune
themselves to Earth influences and forces and with the natural

energies that affect their lives. It is comprised of a set of symbols in the form of an encircled cross'.[9] This basic symbol, the cross of matter within the circle of spirit, occurs across the world and throughout all cultural histories.

The American Indian Medicine Wheel shares similarities with the megalithic stone circles found throughout Europe, but unlike these is generally made of small and portable stones. It can be as simple or as elaborate as you like, but in its essence it represents the Self and also the Source at the centre, the four great paths (as represented by the four directions and the four elements) to the Centre, and the whole encircled by the spiritual powers which shape the universe.

You will need to find twenty-four stones. Look well for these – it may take you a few days to find the right ones, or perhaps you will want to make a trip to a beach or some other specific place and allow yourself the time to hear the right stones call you. It does matter that they feel right – don't just grab any old stone! They must be ones that it will give you pleasure to work with. You can choose twenty-four well-matched ones, or groups of four or eight that are similar to each other in their own group but different from those of the other groups. I have four large flat round ones for the four directions – reddish for the south, black for the west, white quartz for the north and yellowish for the east. In between these to mark the quarter-directions (south-west, north-west and so forth) I place four similar spherical stones. The eight stones that form the inner circle are smaller than the others and well matched. Between this circle and the outer circle I place eight medium-sized flints, two marking each of the four pathways or arms of the cross (see Figure 12).

Set this wheel up in your sacred space, using any preparation ritual that you would normally use before meditation or journeying. As you lay out the wheel, contemplate and acknowledge the symbolic meanings of the directions, the pathways and the centre circle. In many traditions east represents the beginning, dawn, coming into being, so you could start here, and as you place the first stone, meditate on clarity, illumination, the power of the mind, on new beginnings. Or you could start with south, the place of the physical being. Move on round the wheel either clockwise, or in the ascending order of the elements – earth to water, across to air, and up to fire – placing the stones for the four directions first, and

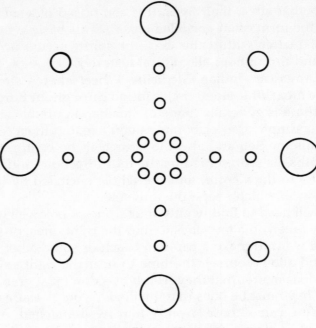

Figure 12

moving then to the quarter-directions. You could then place the inner circle stones, and finally connect the two with the pathway stones. You may want to place in the centre something special, representative of the Self or the Source.

May the fires from the north inspire you
may the winds from the east bring you clarity and illumination
may the scent of summer blossom from the south follow you
may the waters of the west heal and transform you.

EXERCISE: CONTACTING THE FOUR DIRECTIONS

Before you start, read the following exercise through two or three times, so that you are clear about what you are doing. Set up your ritual space as usual. You will need to have at hand a notebook and pen. You will need to take four small pieces of paper and mark a direction on each one, and then place them around you at the four quarters as accurately as you can, allowing yourself about 3 ft from the centre to each direction. During the exercise you will physically move out from the centre to each direction in turn, returning to the centre after each one.

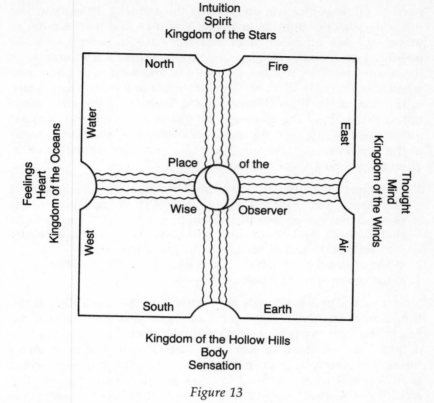

Intuition
Spirit
Kingdom of the Stars

Figure 13

Close your eyes. Take a few minutes to breathe deeply and let go of your day-to-day concerns. When you are ready, see yourself in a beautiful walled garden. It is a still, peaceful, sunny day. At the centre of this garden is a fountain. This is the place of the Wise Observer, the Self. Here at the Centre your talisman is waiting for you, and will accompany you to each direction. From the fountain flow four streams, each to one of the four directions, passing out of the garden through an archway. Stand up (physically, not just in your mind's eye) and move towards the archway in the south. When you reach your piece of paper with 'S' or 'South' written on it, sit down. (Other than this movement to and from the fountain to the four directions, all movement takes place in your imagination.) This direction, this archway, is the gateway to the Kingdom of the Hollow Hills, the direction of earth, sensation and the physical body. The archway is green, and there will be a guardian animal standing beside it – possibly a bear, deer or horse. Take careful note of the animal as you approach it, whether it seems friendly or hostile to you, and how you react to it. Ask the animal what it wants from you, and what you

need to know before you go through the archway. When you feel
ready to, pass through the archway. You may find that in order to
move into this other kingdom you will have to enter a cave, or
possibly pass through a hole in tree-roots. Spend a few minutes in
this earth kingdom, just being quietly in and with your body, and
when you are ready to leave, thank the spirit of the place and return
to the seat of the Wise Observer at the fountain. Now make some
notes. Write about the archway, the guardian animal and your reaction to each other, and any messages. Note down your impressions
of the world through the south archway and your feeling about it.
Then ask yourself these questions:

1. How does the earth part of me, my physical body, feel right now?
   Is it happy with where I am in my life? (It is important in this
   exercise that you answer from the appropriate part of your being –
   that is, don't *think* about how your body feels, but tune directly
   into your body and its sensations for the answers.)
2. What does my body tell me about what I need in my life?
3. What changes could I make to honour my body more?

Next you will move towards the archway in the west. This is the
Kingdom of the Oceans, the place of water, the emotions and the
heart. The archway is blue, and the guardian of this place may be a
dolphin, whale, shark or fish; take careful note of it as it comes
forward to greet you. As before, you will ask what this being wants
from you and what you need to know before passing through this
archway. You may need to dive through the waves to enter this
kingdom. As before, spend a few minutes here being with your
emotional nature, your feelings, and remember to thank the spirit of
the place before leaving. Back at the fountain make your notes as
before, but this time, when asking the three questions, tune into your
feelings and ask and answer them from this perspective only: that is
'How does the water part of me, my emotional life, feel right now?'
And substitute 'feelings' for 'body' in questions 2 and 3.

Repeat this exercise with the other two directions. North is the
Kingdom of the Stars, fire, the place of the creative spirit and intuition. This archway may be guarded by a snake or a phoenix or a
dragon and is red. You may have to jump through flames or pass
between two fires to enter it. The questions will be asked from the
perspective of intuition, the creative spirit, and its perceptions and
needs.

East is the Kingdom of the Winds, air, place of the head, thought.
Its colour is yellow and it may be guarded by an eagle or a hawk, or
perhaps a swallow. You may have to contend with strong winds to
enter. Clearly, the questions for the east revolve around intellectual
thoughts, needs and perceptions. (This doesn't give your intellect

carte blanche to say 'I think this exercise is bullshit – what am I doing this for?' – a common reaction from thinking types! What you are asking for is a rational perspective on where you are in your life right now in general, and whether there are insufficiencies – or excesses – in your intellectual life.)

With each direction, remember to thank the spirit of the place before leaving, and remember to stay with the aspect signified by each direction when asking and answering the questions – body, emotions, intuition and intellect. Remember, too, to return to the place of the Wise Observer each time. You may find that further insight comes from this place.

When you are satisfied that you have noted down all that's necessary, speak quietly to these four aspects of yourself, and make a commitment to honouring any changes that may have come up with regard to your total wellbeing. When you are ready, slowly come back to everyday reality, and ground yourself with food, drink or exercising (use the 'Tree' exercise in Appendix I) as necessary.

A story draws on relationships in the exterior landscape and projects them onto the interior landscape. The purpose of storytelling is to achieve harmony between the two landscapes . . . to reproduce the harmony of the land in the individual's interior. Inherent in story is the power to reorder a state of psychological confusion. . . . The stories had renewed in me a sense of the purpose of my life. This feeling, an inexplicable renewal of enthusiasm after storytelling, is familiar to many people.

Barry Lopez, 'Landscape and Narrative' from
Crossing Open Ground

5

The World of Myth – Some Otherworld Dwellers

Mythology moves towards the soul in the same way that philosophy moves towards the brain.

Robert Bly

As with dreams, myths, legends and fairy tales are not always
what they seem to be. It is too easy to dismiss them as irrele-
vant, childish or simply untrue, or as superstitions more suited
to naive 'primitive' cultures than to modern living. To ignore
them in this way cuts us off from a great wellspring of nourishment, however, as what they actually are is repositories of
wisdom, pictures of inner landscapes as valid and potent as
outer landscapes; while often appearing to depict outer historical or fictitious events they are in fact maps of inner spiritual or
psychological journeys. Myths embody universal truths that
can guide us towards transformation. Because their language is
pictorial, symbolic, they speak to something in us which is
beyond and deeper than the intellect. If we can listen with the
right ears, a myth becomes much more than a simple story; as it
comes alive it becomes the vehicle for profound psychological
or spiritual insight and understanding, and lasting change.

Myths are populated by archetypes; these are the embodiments of underlying universal energy-patterns that shape our
lives, blueprints of the many-faceted aspects of human experience; the forces that manifest themselves in qualities, instincts, characteristics and behaviours that we share with every
other human being, regardless of gender, nationality and conditioning. Archetypes in the personal unconscious speak
through symbols in the individual dream, and in the collective

unconscious through the collective dream, the myth. The symbols will vary from culture to culture, from age to age, and to some extent even from family to family, as although the archetypes are the same, their expression is shaped by the culture in which they are embedded.

Symbols are not the same as signs; they do not stand in for something else. A symbol gives up its meaning gradually; if it is immediately understandable in rational terms it is a sign, not a symbol. Symbols bypass logic and the intellect entirely. They carry great weight and meaning, indeed often a multiplicity of meanings are clustered around a single symbol, and the meanings of a symbol are linked by association rather than by logic. Normally a symbol will evoke a strong emotional response from us at an unconscious level that may well be inexplicable at a rational level.

Each culture has its own set of symbols that convey instantly, and with a great deal more power, what it would need many words otherwise to express. For instance, most of us would understand intuitively the meaning behind a crucifix, a dove, a rose, a swastika, and more recently a yin/yang symbol. Many of these symbols rise up and fall back, culturally, over the ages, or aeons; we are currently coming to the end of the Age of Pisces, a 2000 year period in which the fish, the crucifix and the chalice for instance have been important symbols. Prior to this was the Age of Aries with its own set of symbols, of which the ram was one, and before that the Age of Taurus, with its Mithraic tradition and the bull as a symbol. New symbols gradually come into being; we have yet to see what Aquarius will offer – perhaps a vessel to contain the meeting of the nations. There are other symbols that occur universally, age after age; the cross of matter enclosed by the circle of spirit would appear to be one of these. In the same way, new myths crop up from time to time when a culture is at a point of change; these myths are not 'made up' but born out of the *zeitgeist*.

So symbols are expressions of different archetypal energies. The archetypes personified in the form of visual images give the imagination 'building bricks'. These archetypal beings have enormous power and it is dangerous to identify with them, but approaching them for help and guidance and working with them can be very valuable. (Shape-shifting involves an exchange of energy at a very deep level with these forces; in the uninitiated, however, it can too easily become what we call madness; the borderline is very thin.)

Enormous amounts of energy are tied up in these archetypal images. If this energy is not accessed or expressed somehow, it has a tendency to manifest in disease, discomfort, dispiritedness, disheartedness and depression. The external disorder, confusion and pain we see all around us is a sign that all is not well in the collective, either; the old gods and goddesses need honouring, and we need to return imagery and imagination to the world. Depression is the psyche's way of forcing us down into the world of the unconscious – if we do not go willingly, we are kidnapped like Persephone and held to ransom until we acknowledge whatever it is in our lives that we are not willing to face. Robert Bly suggests that one of the tendencies of New Age thought is to honour higher consciousness, the world of spirit, and dishonour lower consciousness, the world of soul. There is clearly a danger in this, and moreover, since mainstream thought has been doing the same thing for such a long time (at least in its support of the male principle and Logos if not in the more transcendent aspects of higher consciousness, also neglected in our culture), this way of thinking on the part of the New Age movement merely reinforces old patterns. The primitive part of ourselves if left too long in exile becomes exceedingly hungry and ferocious. Working with myth and dream, reintroducing storytelling into our lives, and dance and song are all ways of accessing the energy of the unconscious world. Bly says that 'mythology, connected with the soul, tends to ask you to go down before you go up'. Elsewhere in this book I have mentioned that both journeys need to be made for wholeness, and archetypally speaking the lower world journey, completed first, gives you a strong and rooted foundation for the journey to the upper world.

Mythology, as a map of the psyche, assumes the presence of many different 'people' in the psyche. In myth these manifest as heroes, witches, dragons, dwarves, seventh sons, princesses, frogs and so on. Psychology assumes the same thing; in psychoanalytic language these figures are known as sub-personalities, and working with them can be extremely fruitful, as well as revealing.

In this chapter I want to look at some of the archetypal images in the psyche as they occur as symbols in myths and fairy stories. The following are a random and by no means

comprehensive selection that I have chosen partly with a view
to their common occurrence and their traditional interpretation
and probably largely out of pure favouritism. I cannot possibly
do them justice here; this is intended to be a very brief scan. I
must emphasize that while there are traditionally accepted
'meanings' for these visitors from the Otherworld, I am only
presenting a very simplistic possible interpretation. Only you
will know, over time, what they mean for you. (I must also say
that there are many, many more symbols that are equally important that I haven't mentioned. The Tarot and the I Ching,
for instance, present bodies of knowledge in symbolic form
that some people have devoted their whole life to studying,
and as archetypes the individual images also have their counterparts in myth.)

The symbols, or archetypal beings, that I have chosen to describe are all animate – male and female figures, and animals.
Gods and goddesses, heroes and heroines, witches and giants
and so forth are all aspects of the male and female principles,
and animals as representatives of our instinctual nature are
helpers – power-animals and allies, guides and messengers,
and sometimes also testers and guardians. Even when their
meaning or message is not obvious, their presence in a story or
dream is not accidental or incidental; they are there for a reason
and should be paid attention. Perhaps because we perceive our
world dualistically – male/female, day/night, positive/negative
and so on, the human-type figures of myth tend to come in
pairs (the pairing is James Hillman's observation); psychologically whichever aspect is uppermost or manifest, its counterpart
lies in shadow. If the shadow aspect is not acknowledged too,
it may manifest in our lives in a distorted form. So the princess
has a wicked witch in her shadow; the hero a tyrant; behind the
young man, the Puer, stands an old man, the Senex. The
virtuous wife hides a harlot. If I identify myself with the princess and deny the existence of an inner witch, then eventually
my witchiness will break loose and threaten to devour the
princess – and probably everyone else around, too. (In *Sleeping
Beauty*, the Wicked Fairy was excluded from the birth celebra-
tions, and in her anger at being so ignored, cast the spell that
sent Sleeping Beauty to sleep for one hundred years.) But if
listened to, the witch may turn out to be a helper. One of the
aims of working with myth as I see it is to encourage inner
dialogue, to get the polarities to talk to each other. The path to

wholeness as described in myth needs the shadow-dweller to be acknowledged, accepted and befriended (in the words of Transpersonal Psychology) in order for it to give up the treasure which it invariably carries.

Below are two lists of some of the commonly occurring motifs in myth and fairy tale. The first list consists mainly of human or human-type figures, but I have included a few animals where I feel that their occurrence in myth is so universal that they represent identifiable human attributes, or archetypes beyond just the human realm, such as the male and female principles. Below this list is another one, of animals alone; there is obviously some overlap, and some animals belong in both categories, but generally speaking, the animals in the second list are power-animals, allies or guides to and in the other world, whom we can call upon when we need their particular qualities. Although the distinction may seem academic, to my mind the power-animals have a slightly different function.

Human or human-type figures in myth and fairy tale

King/Queen (also Hero/Heroine) represent the ego, and also the *superior function* in Jungian terminology.

Prince/Princess are symbols of the inner masculine and feminine principles. Often in fairy stories the princess is rescued from a period of sleep, trance or imprisonment – that is to say unconsciousness – by her inner male, the prince. A prince in a fairy story usually has to do battle, undergo strenuous ordeals and often learn the right language before he finally wins his princess, his inner feminine. In both cases they undergo imprisonment, if only in their own imbalance, single-sidedness. Many stories and legends speak to both sexes. If we look, for instance, at Sleeping Beauty as a woman's tale, the woman achieves consciousness when her inner male, or animus, is activated. If we look at it as a man's tale, it is the story of the hero finding and awakening (that is, bringing to consciousness) his inner female, the anima.

The two eldest sons/daughters psychologically are the two *auxiliary functions*.

The Fool is one of my favourite figures. He is the dancer on the edge, the one beyond time. The Fool in the Tarot pack is the unnumbered one, or if you prefer, the one numbered with the circle 0 of eternity. In myth and legend it is almost always the Fool who turns out to be the wise one (he may indeed be the other face of the Wise One), the one who brings home the treasure, to the astonishment of everyone around. The Fool knows what we need for our healing. In myth, the Fool is usually associated with the third (or sometimes seventh) son (and presumably also daughter, though traditionally the Fool is depicted as male – albeit rather androgynous), the overlooked one, the one without apparent or conventional grace, talent, beauty, skills or future. Parsifal, the Holy Fool, the unskilled innocent from apparently humble origins, is one of only three men to achieve the Quest of the Holy Grail. He it is who finally asks the question that sets the waters free and restores fertility to the Wasteland. 'Fools rush in . . .' and this may be their very strength.

There is a connection between the Fool and the Hanged Man in the Tarot. They both symbolize, though differently, the ability to let go of everything, including cherished values and belief-systems, to empty oneself in order for new life to flood in. The Fool overturns the established order, and to this extent he is the anarchist and revolutionary, the herald of the irrational and the unexpected.

Psychologically the Fool is our embedded or inferior function – our less-developed and therefore innocent aspect that actually has direct access to the Treasure-Beyond-All-Price hidden deep in the unconscious.

The Beast is a shadow-function, our undeveloped instinctual and rather frightening animal side that roars at all the wrong moments. It turns into an ally once it's been embraced. It is a symbol of the dark side of the inner male, as the witch is one aspect of the dark side of the inner female.

The Giant (I am grateful to Robert Bly, from one of his taped talks, for the enlightenment he has shed on the giant, the witch and the dwarf in the psyche.) Giants are the large clumsy heavy-handed parts of ourselves that bellow and throw their weight around and tread on people. They, like witches, are always hungry. They seek power, are about inflation and are

the parts of ourselves that are larger-than-life and that bulldoze
less dominant parts/people. They are our overwhelming emotions. They are a bit stupid, and so can be tricked. A distortion
of the male principle.

Witches/wicked fairies/bad stepmothers always have bad press but
are actually crucial to survival. Many of us give our witches
away to other people (projection), which means that we end up
being so 'nice' that we allow ourselves to be victims. Bly says
that mothers often carry our witch for us, and a wife will often
carry her husband's witch for him (as he – and/or her father –
may carry her tyrant). Witches can be harsh and wicked and
ugly but when confronted correctly – face-to-face, fire-to-fire –
they will give back enormous amounts of energy that are yours
by rights. They can represent raw, earthy and sometimes sexual
power. Reclaiming your own witch (or tyrant) will release your
partner or parent to be themselves, and will release you from
the spell of attracting to yourself this particular manifestation of
the distorted feminine principle 'out there'. Witches are generally more cunning and devious than giants, but can also be
tricked – in fact their job involves teaching you to outwit them.

Dwarves are elemental beings who mediate between humans
and nature, or humans and the Otherworld. (Bly says they are
at the interface. We could see them in the same relation between ourselves and nature as the mediaevalists saw angels
between humans and the celestial realm.) They are healers,
and are connected with the mineral kingdom and with the
stars. They know the paths through the Otherworld and can
step in to help abandoned or lost beings. The dwarves are the
little voices that should be listened to. According to Bly the dwarf-
nature is damaged by plastic and other synthetic materials
(and by extension therefore by all substances or actions that act
as insulators against the natural world and its requirements).
They are surely being overwhelmed by our unecological lack of
regard for the planet.

The Wise One represents our innate wisdom, our Higher Self.

Frogs are the much-maligned warty slow parts of ourselves,
denizens of the dark wet places. They represent our instinctual
nature. They are essentially cleansers and healers; they clean

up our psychic garden, ridding it of pests and parasites. They also retrieve lost treasure – remember the princess and the golden ball? When we learn to love their warts we suddenly see that they are in fact beautiful. We all know what they turn into when kissed. They represent an aspect of the inner male.

The Lion represents the Sun, the male principle, the conscious ego. Also power, and sexual and instinctual energy. It is associated with gold. The presence of either a lion or gold in a story points to the male principle.

The Unicorn is associated with the moon, with the female principle, with the unconscious soul. It is connected with emotional energy, with magical powers and receptivity and gentleness, also with the virginal. Its metal and colour is silver.

Dragon/Serpent (These two are not absolutely identical, but are nonetheless, for my purposes, interchangeable. I have treated them here as one beast.) Through the ages it has been feared and revered. It is associated with the primeval raw energy of the land, and of the human being, too – coiled at the base of the spine as kundalini, the fire of the dragon represents the awakening spirit and its movement upwards through the energy-centres of the body, the chakras. The serpent/dragon has long been a symbol of primal energy, power, wisdom, healing (the wand of Caduceus with its two intertwined snakes is still used by the medical profession as a symbol of healing), initiation and transformation. Its ability to shed its outgrown skin is important symbolically.

In China the dragon has always been seen as benevolent, but in the West, largely due to Christianity and its fear of this raw energy (often associated with Eve and therefore womankind) it has become identified with evil, hence the obsession with killing dragons (also killing-off the 'old religion'). The danger with killing it is that unless something equally powerful is put in its place it leaves a deadness of spirit. A more positive way of working with dragon-energy is to give it its due recognition and respect[1] (this prevents it from rampaging all over the place) and then to find a way to channel dragon-power into creative expression. If you suppress it, you will be burned by it. If you acknowledge it and its wisdom, you may ride on its back. Any work of art – music, poetry, painting, dance, performance –

that has the power to move us deeply uses dragon-power. As does sex. As a fire-beast it symbolizes vision, and also guards the treasure-hard-to-find buried deep in the unconscious. (The dragon will also go on the rampage if you attempt to steal, rather than gain honourably, its treasure.) The serpent represents consciousness, and as the worm Ouroboros signifies eternity.

Animals in myth and fairy tale

Bat Letting go; transformation. Trusting the dark, facing your fears. Death and rebirth.

Bear/Badger Hibernatory; comfortable with the dark and the earth. About timing, the willingness to allow things to move at their own pace. Fighting for what is yours; also about dreaming, and going within (or underground) for vision and answers. There is a connection with healing through the use of roots and herbs. The bear is sacred to Artemis, or Diana. As I write this, environmental groups are battling to save the Pyrenean habitat of the last nine brown European bears in France from road-builders.

Boar/Sow Powerful totemic beasts, associated with ferocity, the warrior-nature and vision. The sow is dedicated to the Great Mother; both are in her service.

Bull Male principle, strength, stamina, potency.

Butterfly Transformation, metamorphosis. 'Trusting the process', evolution. Associated with the wind.

Cat Protector, hunter, familiar, guardian. Seer in the dark, walker between the worlds.

Crane/Heron Sacred to gods/goddesses. Associated with hidden wisdom (feet in the water). About secrets and stillness, invisibility.

Crow/Raven Both messengers from the Otherworld. Things not as they seem. Shape-shifting, magic.

Deer Female principle. Gentleness, receptivity, awareness, compassion.

Dog/Hound Humankind's closest animal-companion, and therefore one of the best guides and guardians in and out of the Otherworld. Characteristics: loyalty, fidelity, endurance.

Dolphin Playfulness, compassion, communication, breath, dreaming.

Eagle/Hawk Male principle. Clarity of vision, far-sightedness, objectivity, perspective. Speed of action, decisiveness.

Fox Cunning, camouflage, speed, strategy, timing, observation, discretion.

Goose Being at home in three worlds – water, earth and air. The ability to move between the worlds. It also offers nourishment and in myth it can symbolize the wealth that comes from the earth. A symbol of plenty.

Hare Sacred to the moon-goddess, often appears in North European legend. Feminine principle. Swift, at home in the dark. Otherworld guide, carrier of hidden teachings, women's mysteries.

Horse Another companion animal, strong and trustworthy guide to the Otherworld. Protector. About speed and power.

Mouse Shy, sensitive, concerned with detail. The ability to bite through almost anything to freedom. Hidden watcher.

Otter Playfulness and generosity. 'Going with the flow'.

Owl Wisdom; creature of the night and of the goddess. Teaches that all is not always as it seems. Developing the ability to see in the dark. Sacred to Athena/Minerva.

Salmon is the fish of wisdom and inspiration, in the Pool of Knowledge. If you find yourself swimming against the tide, trust your intuition to lead you to where you need to be. Be prepared to stretch yourself, to leap.

Squirrel Lightness and agility, dancing, looking ahead and preparing what is needed.

Swallow A creature of light, following the sun and so linked with fire and new life. Being prepared to follow where the fire leads you.

Swan Serenity, grace, beauty, acceptance, steadfastness, devotion. Ability to remain centred in the midst of change.

Turtle/Tortoise Pacing/timing; the prudence of steadiness – burying eggs/ideas until their time has come. Retreating inwards when necessary.

Wolf Teacher and leader. Loyal and devoted. Strong sense of both individual and group needs. Allied with moon. Pathfinder.

... we must bring myth back into the realm of subjects suitable for adult consideration. We must learn to accord the inner world described in myth the same respect we give the outer world described by science. When we can understand and accept myth as a living picture of our inner world, we will be on the way to effecting real change.

Robert Johnson, *Ecstasy*

6

Living Mythology – Telling Your Story

> To live mythically means to become aware of your personal and
> collective origins. . . . Personal mythology is . . . the flower on the
> bush, the family myth is the branch, society's conventions form
> the stem, and the root is the human condition.
>
> June Singer[1]

I have noted already that there is a tendency in our society to
view myths as either false beliefs, children's stories or quaint
relics of archaic and primitive cultures, mildly entertaining but
of little value otherwise. Story-telling, however, in its many
different forms, is how accumulated wisdom, crucial to our
psychological and spiritual well-being if not our actual existential survival, is preserved and passed down through the generations. We find in the world's great myths blueprints for the
journeys we make individually and collectively in the course of
our 'earthwalk'. And mythology is alive and kicking – John
Matthews, in *The Celtic Shaman*, observes: '. . . these mythic
events are still happening, and will continue to occur as long as
there are those who acknowledge the power of these archetypal stories'. Moreover, whether we are conscious of it or not,
mythology still plays a large determining part in how we
actually live our lives. June Singer in the foreword to Feinstein
and Krippner's book *Personal Mythology*[2] says:

> Personal Myths structure our awareness and point us in the
> direction that becomes our path. If we are unacquainted with the
> contents of our personal mythology we are carried by it uncon-
> sciously, with the result that we confuse what exists objectively
> in the world with the image of the world supplied to us by our
> own distorted lenses.

81

Feinstein and Krippner[3] define a personal myth as:

> a constellation of beliefs, feelings, and images that is organized
> around a core theme. . . . Personal myths explain the world,
> guide personal development, provide social direction, and
> address spiritual longings in a manner that is analogous to the
> way cultural myths carry out these functions for entire societies.
> . . . Your personal mythology may be thought of as the system of
> complementary and contradictory personal myths that organizes
> your sense of reality and guides your actions.

They go on to say that an individual's central theme is a compo-
site one, constructed from a variety of sources. It will be shaped
by the prevailing myths of both the immediate and societal
cultural environment of the individual, merged with values
and belief-systems held by the family, coloured by the individual's own temperament and life-experiences, added to by
images provided by peers, teachers, role-models (heroes and
anti-heroes), and subject to the influences of the media. While
each person's core mythology remains unique, much insight
can be gained by an exploration of the archetypal themes
underlying some of our behaviours as they appear in myth.

Now the core theme for an individual is unlikely to actually
be a myth in the sense that we are using the word in this book.
That is to say, it is probably not an actual fairy story or legend
that has distinctly recognizable archetypal themes. What it is
likely to be is a prevailing and unarticulated belief or constel-
lation of beliefs that govern/s our behaviour and direction in
the world. Uncovering this central theme frees us to change it if
we feel that it no longer serves us. So what I am looking at in
this chapter is a way of accessing this core theme through
myth.

As I have said, myths speak to every aspect of the human
condition. They act as keys. On this premise, there is likely to
be a myth in the collective that has a bearing on the issues
central to an individual's life. There may, indeed, be several
relevant myths; they may be complementary or contradictory;
some may serve you, others may not. I am suggesting that a
recognition of the stories we heard as children that still have a
strong 'pull' for us, which draw us strongly or move us in some
way, have a connection with our core theme.

Because myths speak so powerfully to our subconscious
minds, they have the ability to both limit us and free us,
depending on the myth, and also on how strongly we identify

with it – albeit unconsciously. We may find ourselves living-out, without realizing it, our own personal variations of stories we heard as children. Whether they are tragic stories such as 'The Little Mermaid' and 'The Red Shoes', questing stories such as 'Sir Gawain and the Green Knight', or happily-ever-after stories such as 'Cinderella' or 'Sleeping Beauty', their effect is to shape impressionable young minds and their tendency is to form the foundation of adult values and beliefs. This is a double-edged sword; while their effects are powerful, and their messages crucially important, we have mislaid in our culture the wisdom to know for ourselves and to pass on to our children the fact that these are all *metaphors of an inner journey, our own inner journey*; with this vital information missing, even though we are not aware we are doing it, our tendency is to see the outer world through the lens of these early images, so that Cinderella looks for her prince 'out there', Gawain does battle 'out there', the Little Mermaid exchanges her fishy tail for marriage vows and a microwave, and so forth. That is not to say that Cinderella's partner does not exist in the outer world, or that Gawain doesn't ever run into trouble in 'real life', or that the Little Mermaid won't have to leave, to some extent, her own watery home in order to make a relationship; just that, first and foremost, these journeys are meetings with our inner lovers, partners, demons, enemies; and to live them out, un-consciously, Out There can lead to unnecessary confusion and suffering.

There is a self-fulfilling quality to these myths; as long as their theme remains unconscious you are likely to live out their messages over and over. The inner and outer worlds reflect each other. If your inner world is in a state of conflict or turmoil, your outer world, through projection, is likely to be, too. And, of course, introjection works in reverse; we know through research done that if a person is told enough times that s/he is dumb, or backward or clever or lazy or ineffective, eventually the message will be internalized and that person will become dumb/backward/clever or whatever. Children in a family or school situation who are consistently praised for their intelligence will tend over time to do better academically than those of the same initial intellectual calibre who are put down or ridiculed as stupid. Situations in which they then find them-selves will tend to reinforce that belief, as we tend to create environments and make choices that confirm what we believe about ourselves and the world. So finding a myth that represents our personal belief-system can help us in identifying where we are stuck, as well as giving us the option of redrawing our maps.

THE WOUND

We are all, to some extent and in some way, wounded. It is part of our humanness, just as being human also encompasses the urge towards wholeness. When and in what way our wound occurs is unique to each of us. There are many small wounds; each of us will also have one or more major wounds, which, if left unhealed, will constitute a 'sticking-place' for us. They also, like the grain of sand in the oyster, will contain or motivate our urge to healing, that which we need to learn in order to effect our wholeness, to find and offer our unique treasure to the world.

Our wound may occur very early on. It might be a birth or even pre-birth trauma. Many wounds occur in childhood; a primary relationship that didn't work – perhaps a devouring or rejecting mother, a violent or absent father, the loss of an important loved one or friend. The birth of a sibling may be enough, or entry into what feels like a hostile school. The first time a grown-up lies to you, or an incidence of bullying; perhaps an experience of getting lost.

Adolescence can be another acutely painful time, with all its emotional upheavals, first love, meeting with loss, peer-group pressure and the need to belong. Many adolescents are confronted, too, with a sense of alienation and despair at what we have done to the world. Despite the apparent 'coolness' of teenagers, many of them have such clear vision, such a sensitivity to the world around them and its fragility and its beauty that it is almost too painful to handle. This may be a time, too, when a young human first encounters the numinous, a transcendent or visionary experience of great beauty, the sense of limitless potential, the apparent loss of which may haunt their adult life unless they are able to find a vehicle or container for this sense of awe and mystery, this brief glimpse of the vastness and power of the universe.

And then there are the wounds of adulthood; again the wounds of love and loss and unmet dreams and hopes, also of belonging and of aloneness, and the existential questions of meaning and meaninglessness. Mid-life brings these issues closer into focus as we balance on the edge of different perceptions and perspectives, a shifting perhaps of values and the accompanying sense of transition, transience and uncertainty, of mortality.

It may be that we come into this world wounded; it may be, instead, that our movement away, psychologically and physically, from the experience of oneness, primarily with its mother and the immediate environment, of the baby and the very young infant constitutes a deep wounding. Perhaps the wound is our sense of ungodliness; the discrepancy between what we might be and what we actually are, or perceive ourselves to be. Much of our struggle would then seem to be separation-anxiety; not just as spoken of by clinical psychology, but a deeper intuited sense that we are alienated from our divine origins, our star-fire nature. This may be at the same time both the original wound, and that which drives us on. There can, of course, be no easy answers for this type of wound, though this question remains central to the spiritual search.

Astrology once again can shed light both on where in the individual's life significant wounds may occur (the placement of Saturn by house, sign and aspect may be helpful), and to illuminate times of crisis, which are also times of opportunity for growth. For instance, astrology tells us that there are classic times in each person's life when we feel pulled, or drawn, to make major changes; when the scar-tissue over the wound itches more insistently, when the 'veil between the worlds' seems thinner and the winds of change blow more keenly. In short, 'do or die' times. These times of change may lead up over several months of a year or more to the crisis point, and the repercussions will be felt for an equally long time afterwards. Astrology tells us that one of these times is around the age of twenty-eight, the 'Saturn return' time, when transiting Saturn – the dweller on the threshold, guardian of the gate – returns to its natal position on the birthchart to shine a light into your dark places. Many people enter – or leave – a marriage or long-term relationship during this period, or have a baby, or change careers or countries. Even if the outward change is not this obvious, subtle but powerful changes in the psyche seem to take place around this time; a skin is shed, and the person that emerges is subtly different from the person before. Astrology also tells us that you may have, as it were, a second bite at the cherry at around the age of forty-two (astrologically marked by the mid-points of both Saturn and Uranus. There is a further Saturn return at around fifty-six.) This is a time when many people pause, take stock and do a turnaround in their lives, hopefully to realign themselves more closely with their life's purpose. Some do it more dramatically than others, but most people are aware of an itching, a restlessness, a need to breathe different air, look upon different scenery. This is a good time, if you haven't done it before, to take a closer look at the wound, at your hurting places; to invite them in for tea, as a sage once said.

HEALING THE WOUND

In the rest of this chapter I am going to look at ways of starting to identify and then heal some of our wounds through working with myth. As with the rest of the book, these are only suggestions; I have found them to be effective and you might like to try them.

There are many, many different fairy tales and myths. They are all teaching tales. Many of them deal with a primal wound, and of these, the healing (or heroic) myths also teach us how to heal that wound, how to turn the grain of sand into the pearl. A tragic myth tends not to offer this healing salve. It is obviously helpful to know which 'your' myth is (or myths are), and what you can do about it if the myth itself doesn't appear to offer healing.

Clarissa Pinkola Estes in her wonderful book[4] has this to say about myth (she is writing for women in her book, but though the nature, tests, and dangers of male and female journeys differ, the distinction between heroic and tragic dramas applies to both):

> The heroic drama begins with a heroine on a journey. Sometimes she is not psychologically awake. Sometimes she is too sweet and doesn't perceive danger. Sometimes she has already been mistreated and makes the desperate moves of a captured creature. However she begins, the heroine eventually falls into the clutches of whatever or whoever, and is sorely tested. Then, through her wit and because she has people who care for her, she is freed and stands taller as a result.

In a tragedy the heroine is snatched, forced, or drives straight into hell and is subsequently overwhelmed with no-one to hear her cries, or else her pleas are ignored. She loses hope, loses touch with the preciousness of her life, and collapses. Instead of being able to savour her triumph over adversity, or her wisdom of choices and her endurance, she is degraded and deadened. *. . . But there is good news. The way to change a tragic drama back into a heroic one is to open the secret, speak of it to someone, write another ending, examine one's part in it and one's attributes in enduring it.* [my emphasis]

The kind of work I have been doing in my workshops hinges on this vital difference between heroic and tragic myth. The actual approach appears to be very simple, and the results can be profound, and often immediate; just the recognition that you have been stuck, that you can choose change, that you can re-write your ending releases creative energy, although interestingly the breaking of a spell, an enchantment, may first of all bring extreme exhaustion, followed only later by a sense of freedom and elation.

TELLING YOUR STORY

If at all possible, for this part of your work you need to have a witness – someone to hear you, to be there for you, to 'hold the threads' as you untangle and reweave them. Apart from the objective, practical and supportive role of this person, a witness to your life story – for this is what it is, at least in part – adds power and dimension and liberation to the work. If it is absolutely impossible for you, then the next best thing is to tell your story to a tape-recorder, and the third best is to write it.

Though the actual telling requires little time – anything from half-an-hour to one-and-a-half hours – you will need some time ahead of it, and how much work you do afterwards is up to you. I'm still working with my story several years later. Perhaps there is never a point when you know the work to be completed.

You will need to start by finding a myth, your myth, calling it to you. You may know instantly what story belongs to you, or you may have a strong memory of one or more fairy stories from your childhood to which you were particularly drawn. Once you set the wheels in motion, you may find that the myth comes to you, either in your waking life in some form, or in dream. Or you may need to go through several books of myth or fairy story before you find one that speaks to you. It is important not to analyse it, and it is equally important, if you have to go to a book for it, not to memorize it verbatim.

You might like to give yourself the time to go through various story books. If you don't have children, and therefore no children's books at hand, spend an afternoon in the library. Choose collections of traditional fairy stories or legends rather than modern stories (although there are some more recent writers, like Oscar Wilde, who have written powerful stories). Generally speaking, books where the stories have been collected from a folk or oral tradition have sufficient archetypal elements, handed on down through the generations, to speak to us strongly at a subliminal level; besides, these are the ones you are likely to have been read as a child. The Grimm brothers' collections have some fine, if grisly, material; there is also Hans Christian Andersen. (Robert Bly considers his stories to be misogynist; however, since we live in a patriarchal culture, many stories are. This in fact may add to their power for our purposes here, especially if you are a woman. Just be careful what myths you read when you look for healing ones, though.) The 'Arabian Nights' collection is another possibility. On second thoughts, give yourself several afternoons! You may need to check out stories from your own ethnic background, if you are not Anglo-Saxon; remember, too, that the Celtic tradition, and the Norse, are just as likely to be in your race-memory if you are British.

Three further things I should mention here. The first is that you may not find your story this way. You may put down the books feeling that nothing held you. It's almost certain, though, that having fed your imagination in this way, your unconscious will oblige with an appropriate myth or story within a day or two.

Another thing is that, occasionally, a myth will speak to you so strongly when you look at it in this light that you may experience it in quite a dramatic way. This has happened to various people I know; one woman, as she read through 'Thumbelina', felt herself to be very small, very frightened and in a rather dark place. Working through the myth later showed her where in her life she had become trapped; how she had agreed to enter a relationship that kept her from the light and the air. (Thumbelina has a positive ending, which gave her hope.) Another person experienced the equivalent of a nettle-rash as she realized her anger at the injustice of the 'Seven Swans' story, where a trapped princess has to knit, in an impossible amount of time, seven shirts out of nettles in order to free her brothers. This indicated where her work lay. And one of my workshop participants had chosen a classic love story as 'her' myth. As she knew it, though, the story ended with the tragic parting of the couple. She learned that day that, in fact, the original myth had a happy ending; and the same evening, met the man who is now her partner. Your response may be altogether less dramatic – I use these examples really to show the power of myth.

The third thing is that the story doesn't necessarily have to have a tragic ending. If it offers healing, hope, a blessed marriage, all well and good. The best stories offer a solution to the ordeals and dilemmas they present, which are after all dramatic representations of the experiences most of us have to one degree or another here on this earth. If, however, it is a 'happy' story, there is no need for you to follow the steps given below for tragic endings.

The next step is simple, but be prepared for it to be more powerful than it sounds as if it will be. The telling can be very emotional. Take yourself, and your companion if you are working with someone, to your sacred space, and prepare both the physical place and yourself as usual for a meditation or visualization. You may want to start in your sanctuary. You can choose to sit or lie; lying down is closer to the unconscious and therefore more powerful; you are also likely to feel more vulnerable. Sometimes, too, the brain gets its messages muddled, and you may fall asleep – especially if there is something you want to avoid! In either case, don't start until you are deeply relaxed, and sure of being uninterrupted. You will tell the myth or story you have chosen with your eyes closed, *in the first person, and in the present tense*, and as you remember it. It is important that in the telling you do not try to analyse, interpret or compare events in the story with events in your own life. You are telling the story as you remember it. If in the telling you miss bits out, add bits in or if there is a muddle between 'real' life and fairy story, that's fine. It's all grist to the mill, and it is in these apparent 'stumbles' that the life of the story, and its keys, live for you. So tell it as it comes, without thought.

If you have a witness, his or her role is to note down all the key incidents and passages exactly as you tell them (bear in mind that you may need to talk slowly.) It is tremendously helpful if your witness can also make notes about the way you tell the story; facial expressions, body-language and gestures, hesitation or muddle, repetition, emotion, forgetfulness, a slip into the third person. The witness should not comment or interrupt in any way except to ask for clarification or repetition if necessary. He or she should also not at any stage attempt to interpret or analyse the story for you. His or her role is to witness only.

Once you have told your story, your witness is to read it back to you exactly as they noted it down, again with no comment or embellishments except to tell you anything he or she noticed about the way in which you told it as recommended above. When the witness has finished, keep the notes, and take a break, with a grounding exercise (e.g. the 'Tree' in Appendix I) if necessary, and something to eat or drink.

If you are telling your story to a tape-recorder, obviously you will miss out on the visual feedback, but you may pick up quite a lot from the tone of your voice and from hesitations and breaks. It will be helpful to transcribe the story from the tape – it is well worth the effort. Once again, even if as you write you think of a better or different way of putting something or remember a bit you missed out, resist the impulse to alter the original. Make a note of it elsewhere if you want. If you are writing the story, write it through without pausing and without thinking about it as you go. Just write. Whichever method you use, be gentle with yourself for the rest of the day.

WORKING WITH YOUR STORY

Over the next few hours, or days, there are various things you need to do. If you want to check your version of the story against the original, do; it can be very helpful to see where the two diverge, as they probably will. Don't amend yours; just notice. Spend some time, too, isolating details that seem important, and consider what these might reflect in your own life. Now is the time to look at the differences and similarities between your own past and the story; you may want to write an abridged version of your life to compare the two. Pay particular attention to the ending of the myth; are you happy with it? How much of a hold does it have over you? In what way would you change it if you were writing that fairy story? Is the myth a healing myth or a tragic one? How many of the characters in it have counterparts in your life? In yourself?

The next step is to encapsulate your own interpretation of the myth in a sentence. If your myth is a healing one, with a resolution that seems right and positive, this is as far as you need to go. Use your sentence to celebrate, as an affirmation of where your life is working for you at times when you feel you need a little reminding. If, however, your myth is a tragic one, think carefully about the message this myth holds for you. It may be something like: 'whatever I do, it's never enough'; 'it's my destiny to be a loser'; 'women (men) in my family tend to have unhappy marriages'; 'men (women) always break your heart'; 'I don't deserve anything better than this' and so on.

The next step is to create a counter-myth. There are various ways of doing this, and you may feel you'd like to try all of them! One way is to actively look for a healing myth that you like. Read it over and over to yourself until you have it to hand, and can write it out without needing to check details. Another way is to create for yourself an affirmative statement that counters the negative message, *and which you use every time you catch yourself falling back into the old patterning*. Your counter-statement could be something along the lines of: 'I'm doing the best I can, and that's good enough', or 'I deserve the best life can offer me', or 'moment by moment I'm creating a loving relationship' – whatever you need to hear about and for yourself. Say this affirmation quietly to yourself whenever you remember. At first you may feel some resistance; perhaps it feels silly, or just untrue, but if you say it enough times you breathe life into it and eventually give it wings. And the third way, which may take you ages – it's taken me years – is to re-write the original myth with an ending that you want to live with. You may need to throw off the 'fated' feeling that you 'shouldn't' be changing the ending, or you may feel that your first attempts are pretty limp. But persevere – whose life is it, anyway?

EXERCISE: DRAWING YOUR LIFELINE

You will need a large sheet of paper for this; architect's paper works well, or tape two or three sheets of A4 or A3 paper together. Choose some paints or coloured pens. Give yourself enough time and space to take as long as you need; probably a minimum of one hour.

You are going to draw a 'road-map' of your life up until this point. Starting from birth, draw a line to represent your journey to where you are now. You may find that your road is a broad smooth highway with very few contours or changes of direction, or it may be a very tortuous narrow track with constantly changing scenery either side. Sketch in whatever landmarks and views present themselves. As you draw, take note of whether it has been a bumpy ride, exciting if stressful, or whether it's been smooth and largely uneventful. You will need to choose two coloured pens, one for the good times, and one for the traumas. Mark the good times in a joyful colour with a circle by the side of the road, and the bad times with a cross in an appropriate colour. Write also at each of these points the names of people and also the qualities in yourself who/which gave you the support you needed to pull yourself through the bad times, or who shared in your good times. Mark in everything of importance – losses, achievements, deaths, pleasures, illnesses, people entering or leaving your life, birth of siblings, offspring, important journeys and transitions. When you have completed your map right up until now, sit back and look at it. Acknowledge the good times with thanks, and as you scan the crosses of the bad times, make a promise to yourself to make time to grieve over, heal and let go of old unhealed wounds. You may want to set up some grieving time for yourself when you quietly bring these times back to mind before giving them a ritual burial in whatever manner seems right to you. Perhaps you will write an account of one or more of these painful times before burning the paper and scattering the ashes; perhaps you will find you need to talk to someone of some of this pain before you can let it go; perhaps you need to walk by the sea while acknowledging both the old wound and the fact that you are ready to let it go. Whatever you choose to do, be gentle with yourself and hold in your mind the fact that you have come through.

And lastly, turn your large sheet of paper over and draw for yourself an ideal future road-map, marking in the scenery you would like to have, the kind of events you would like to have happen for you, and the people you would like to travel with. Mark in old and unlived dreams, as well as new untried possibilities. Let your imagination create for you your dream future life. When you have marked in all you can think of, write in bold colourful letters your affirmative statement about the way your life is going to be for you from now on.

PART II

Transformational Journeys

'The story is like the wind,' a bushman called Zhabbo said. 'It comes from a far-off place and we feel it.'

Laurens van der Post, *A Far-Off Place*

The world is patterned for our freedom.
The ladders start here.

Stephen Parr, *After the Ice*

The Story of Psyche and Eros

Once upon a time, in another country, lived a king and queen and their three very beautiful daughters. The two eldest daughters were stunning, but the youngest, Psyche, was indescribably lovely, more beautiful than anything in existence – the sun, the moon or the fairest flower. So beautiful, in fact, that as time went on, thousands of people were making pilgrimages over land and sea to worship her. She was seen as the Goddess of Love incarnate, and people started to pay to her the kind of homage that was due only to the immortal Venus, whose shrines started to fall into disrepair, whose festivals were forgotten, whose altars were left unswept.

Eventually, of course, Psyche incurred the wrath and jealousy of the Goddess Venus. She called her son, Eros, to her, told him the whole story, and implored him to wound Psyche with his infamous arrows, so that she would fall desperately in love with the vilest, most degraded, monstrous outcast of a man to be found on the face of the earth.

Psyche, meanwhile, was feeling miserable, lonely and rather ill. Far from being flattered by the adulation of the people, she began to hate the beauty that so raised her above everyone else that no one dared to court her or propose to her. Her two sisters were long married, but she was still at home, single.

Her father, who was beginning to fear that the gods might be angry with him for allowing his subjects to pay so much attention to his daughter, decided to go to the ancient oracle of Apollo to ask where he was to find a husband for Psyche. The oracle told him that Psyche was to be led to a high mountain where she must be left. There she would be wed to a dreadful dark immortal being.

Despite the parents' grief and protestations, the oracle had to be obeyed. All was made ready for the terrible wedding, and amidst weeping and wailing the procession moved towards the chosen crag. Psyche alone accepted her destiny and walked resolutely forwards and upwards, until she reached the top.

There she was left alone sobbing and trembling, awaiting her fate, while the crowd slowly and in enormous sorrow proceeded back down to their homes. The broken-hearted king and queen shut themselves up in their palace behind closed doors and darkened windows.

Psyche, however, was befriended by the west wind, which sprang up out of nowhere, swelled her garments and floated her off the ground into a valley at the foot of the hill where she was gently laid on the softest flowery turf, where she fell asleep. When she awoke, she calmly followed a stream to the centre of a wood where she came upon a royal palace, too exquisite to be anything other than the dwelling-place of a god. Psyche, entranced by its beauty, timidly entered, and was greeted by a disembodied voice that told her that the treasures were all hers, and that anything she desired was hers for the asking. Baths were run for her by invisible serving-maids, a bed was made, and after Psyche had rested she was told by the voice, amidst heavenly music, that the wedding feast was awaiting her. After all these delights Psyche, exhausted, went to her room and again lay down on her bed.

Around midnight she heard a gentle male voice whispering. Psyche at first was frightened, but her new and invisible husband reassured her as he climbed into bed beside her. He took her into his arms, and with loving tenderness they passed the night. But just before daybreak he left her hastily, before the light returned to show her his face.

For the next 3 or 4 days, this was the pattern. By day Psyche was on her own in the palace, where her every need and desire was attended to. She could not feel lonely with so many voices directed to her total comfort. After dark, her tender, if invisible, lover would join her until daybreak.

Meanwhile back in Psyche's old country, the king and queen remained inconsolable. News of her sad fate had spread, and her sisters, living in distant cities with their husbands, hastened to comfort their parents.

On the night of their arrival, Psyche's lover, whom she still only knew by touch and voice, warned her that she was in deadly danger from her own sisters, and told her that if they appeared on the rock from which Psyche had disappeared, presumed dead, then she was to pay no attention to their mourning. If she did, it would cause him tremendous unhappiness, and totally destroy her. Psyche promised him that she would obey his word, but when she found herself alone again the next morning, her strength deserted her. She suddenly felt herself to be totally alone, trapped in this vast palace without any human company save for an invisible and elusive lover, and now forbidden to see her own sisters. She spent the day sobbing, and could not stop even when her lover joined her in bed. In the end her pleas persuaded him to let her see her sisters, though he warned her that it would be quite disastrous. He said that her sisters were evil-minded women who would try to force her to discover what he looked like. On no account was she to listen to them or talk to them of him. After Psyche had embraced and kissed and caressed him and promised him her undying love and loyalty, he softened and said that she might show them the palace and even make them gifts, so long as she remembered her promise. He also told her that she was with child, and that the child would be born a god if she kept her word, but a mortal if she betrayed him. And so Psyche had the west wind blow her sisters down.

Her sisters were consumed with jealousy when they saw Psyche's situation. Their initial joy at finding her alive and well soon turned to envy and bitterness, and they started to question Psyche about her lover. On their first visit, Psyche told them briefly that he was a handsome young man who spent his days out hunting. But on the second visit she forgot what she had said the first time and said that he was a middle-aged merchant. Naturally the sisters started to get suspicious, and started to wonder if perhaps Psyche hadn't actually ever seen him, and if, therefore, her lover was a god. The idea of their sister not only being wed to a god but also carrying a god-child inflamed their envy until it became intolerable, and together they conceived a plan for Psyche's downfall. The next time they visited, they told Psyche that she had married a monster, a dreadful serpent whose debauched appetites included a predilection for devouring heavily pregnant women. They told her that this monster had been seen in neighbouring hills in the daytime, slithering home to the palace at dusk, and naturally he wouldn't want Psyche to see him.

For the rest of the day, Psyche tried to dispel these fears from her mind, but she could not forget what her sisters had said, and that night, she determined to follow their advice. Many times her lover had warned her that if she tried to see what he looked like disaster would follow and she would lose him forever, but now her fear was too much to bear, and remembering her sisters' advice, she prepared an oil-lamp by which to see him, and a carving-knife to plunge into his throat. After their love-making that night, so loving and tender that she almost dismissed her fears, Psyche lay quietly until she judged that her lover was asleep, and then she crept out of bed, stole to where she had hidden the lamp and knife, and returned with the lamp held high.

For a full minute she stood still in total disbelief and wonder. In her bed lay the most beautiful man she had ever seen, so beautiful that surely he must be a god. And then from the corner of her eye she caught sight of a quiver of arrows. These could only belong to Eros, the god of love. Wonderingly she stretched out her hand to touch the tip of one of them, pricked herself on its sharpness, and instantly fell in love with Love himself. In joy and desire, she fell upon her sleeping lover's breast, kissed his lips, caressed his downy white wings (for he was after all a god), and in her eagerness and pleasure she spilt a drop of oil from the lamp and scalded his shoulder. In a flash Eros awoke, took in the scene, turned reproachful and angry eyes on his wife and told her that she had lost him forever with her betrayal and disobedience. With that he flew off and up into the heavens, soon to be lost from sight.

Psyche, left behind, was devastated. Eros' final words to her were that it was for her sake that he had disobeyed the orders of his mother, Venus, and instead of inflaming her with passion for some unworthy outcast, had taken the risk of becoming her lover himself, but despite his repeated gentle warnings, Psyche had brought them both to their doom.

Psyche in her sorrow tried to kill herself, stunned by this double blow of the loss of Eros and the exposure of her sisters' trickery. Her attempt was unsuccessful, though, and she fell into aimless wandering.

Eventually, as luck would have it, she arrived at the palace of her eldest sister. Psyche was no longer the innocent young maiden she had been only a few days before. She saw her chance for revenge and told her sister what had happened, but added that Eros, after being discovered, had told her that because of her, Psyche's, betrayal, he was going to take her eldest sister as his bride in her place, and whistled up the west wind to take Psyche away. The wind had deposited her here.

The sister, her whole being aflame with greed and desire,

immediately rushed off to tell her husband some story about her parents having just died, and set sail at once for the mountain where she had in the past been carried by the west wind into Psyche's palace. She neglected to notice that a different wind altogether was blowing when she reached the crag, and jumping off in total confidence was dashed to pieces on the rocks below.

Meanwhile Psyche wandered on, until arriving at another city, she recognized the palace as being that of her second sister. She told this sister the same story, and this sister came to suffer the same fate.

As Psyche continued her travels through country after country searching for her lost love, Eros was lying in his mother's royal suite with severe burns to his bow-drawing shoulder. All hell had broken loose in the heavens when Venus heard the scandal surrounding her son's disobedience, and when she realized exactly who it was with whom her son had become intimate, her fury knew no bounds. She stormed through the heavens vowing eternal revenge by annihilation on Psyche, and persuaded Mercury, the winged messenger, to use all his powers to discover Psyche's whereabouts.

At around the same time, Psyche was being offered the advice of the goddess Juno, who suggested that her only chance of survival was to make a voluntary surrender to Venus. She also pointed out that the wounded Eros was quite likely to have flown home to his mother.

Simultaneously with Mercury posting his reward-for-information notices, Psyche, with all the courage she could muster, arrived at Venus' gates, where she was met and cursorily dragged into the lady Venus' presence. Venus shrieked with anger and hysterical laughter to see her and sent her off for torture. When the poor battered Psyche was hauled back into her throne-room, Venus herself set upon her, tearing out handfuls of hair and shredding her clothes.

Then she set her four seemingly impossible tasks.

First she had placed in front of the girl an enormous heap of mixed grains – wheat, barley, millet, lentils, beans, poppy and vetch, and told her that she was to sort it all into its separate varieties by nightfall. Psyche, weary and bloodied, just sat numbly gazing at the mountain of grain, knowing there was no chance of sorting it herself by dusk. But within minutes an ant, chancing to pass by, took pity on Psyche and rallied every ant in the district to come and help. Working furiously they sorted the pile grain by grain until by Venus' return at nightfall the task was done.

Venus, however, was not satisfied. She didn't believe that Psyche had completed the task herself and determined to set her a harder one the next day.

At dawn she called the girl to her and pointed to a field of golden sheep wandering the other side of a river. She told Psyche that she was to gather a handful of their precious wool. Psyche descended to the stream, but with the sole intention of throwing herself into it to end her sorrows. But a green reed, of the sort used by Pan for his pipes (Psyche had met Pan before, on her departure from Eros' palace) was blown upon by a divine breeze, and whispered to her that she was not to kill herself. It also warned her that she should not approach the sheep until twilight, as the fierce sun so inflamed the sheep that they became lethally dangerous to any human who approached. However, at sundown they became docile and submissive and she would be able to pass them by and collect the wisps of golden fleece caught on the brambles. Psyche listened to the reed, and was able to return that evening with an armful of golden wool.

Venus grinned maliciously, and set her yet another, yet more difficult, task. She was given a crystal jar, and told to dip it into the very centre of the dark and icy river Styx at the point where it burst out of the rock on its journey to the Underworld. The river was guarded by fierce dragons, and the source at the rockface was impossibly steep and slippery. The task was so overwhelming that Psyche was past even crying. There seemed no way of escaping with her life.

However, the sharp eyes of an eagle from Jupiter (who owed Eros a favour) spotted Psyche's trouble, took the jar from her, dodged the rows of poisoned fangs and forked tongues and filled it from the centre of the river Styx.

Venus was still not appeased, and set Psyche the most difficult task of all. She was to take a little box down to the underworld death-palace of Pluto, and ask Queen Proserpine to fill it with her beauty-ointment for Venus. Psyche saw that she was being sent to her death, and despairing once more, she decided to hasten the process for herself by throwing herself off a high tower.

By this time, Psyche was becoming accustomed to expecting

the unexpected, so it was not a total surprise when the tower suddenly burst into speech. It pointed out to her that if she were to kill herself now, then there was no chance of return from the Underworld, but if she were to listen to it, the tower, it could not only tell her the shortest way in to the Underworld but also how to get back out alive.

Its advice was as follows: she was to take two pieces of barley-bread with honey, one in each hand, and two coins in her mouth. The coins were for her passage across the river Styx, one each way; the ferryman was to take them directly from her mouth. The bread was to be thrown on entry and exit to Cerberus, the three-headed hound who guarded the gateway to the Underworld – while the three heads quarrelled over the bread she could slip past. On no account was she to let fall the coins or the bread – if she did there would be no return. Her most difficult task, however, would be to harden her heart to the pleas for help from the needy people she would pass – a lame man with his lame ass whose load had fallen; the body of a drowning man floating past in the river with his arm raised for help; three women (the three Fates) needing extra hands for spinning and weaving cloth. She was warned that these would all be traps set by Venus to which she must not yield. Nor, once there, must she accept a comfortable chair and a magnificent feast. She was to sit on the ground and accept only bread (remember how Proserpine (or Persephone) in accepting the pomegranate seeds sealed her fate in the Underworld). Her last temptation would be to open the box of ointment that she would be bringing back. This, too, she must resist.

Psyche thanked the tower and set off, and, spurred on by the knowledge that her life depended on it, fulfilled her task, right up to the last detail, despite the fact that it nearly broke her heart to ignore the pleas for help from other human beings. But then, on the last stretch, out of the Underworld and on her way back to Venus, her curiosity compounded by her desire to steal a little of the beauty-ointment overcame her, and she opened the box.

As far as she could see, the box was empty. However, out slunk a cloud of Stygian sleepiness that overpowered her, so that she fell motionless to the ground.

But she had made the return journey and the tides of fortune had turned in her favour. It so happened that Eros, now recovered, escaped that day from the prison of his mother's palace, and unable to bear his separation from Psyche any longer, set out to find her, and having done so, with great care brushed away the cloud of sleep and returned it to its box. He roused Psyche, embraced her with joy, and sent her off to Venus with her ointment. He, meanwhile, sped off to Jupiter (who had a soft spot for him) and pleaded with him to intercede for him with Venus. Jupiter diplomatically gave Psyche to drink of the nectar that would render her immortal (thus establishing her as Eros' equal) and declared to the assembled gods and goddesses that it was high time Eros was married, if only to keep him out of mischief and restrain him from shooting indiscriminate arrows into unsuspecting hearts. The whole of the heavens agreed, a sumptuous wedding-feast was prepared, and Psyche and Eros were ceremoniously married.

And in due course, Psyche bore a child, a daughter, whose name was Pleasure.[1]

7

The Heroic Quest

We seek not rest but transformation.

Marge Piercy[1]

Any journey of significance will leave you changed. This is as
true of the inner plane as it is of the outer. Even if you come
back to the same place, you will no longer be the same person.
Or rather, to embrace the Eastern love of paradox, you will be
'the same, and yet not the same'. The place you return to, too,
will look different.

> We shall not cease from exploration
> And the end of all our exploring
> Will be to arrive where we started
> And know the place for the first time.[2]

Through our lives we make many journeys, and if we see each
journey as a circular section of a spiral progression, then it is
easy to see how our perspective and perception will change
with each turn as we view our world from what is, and yet is
not quite, the same point.

Joseph Campbell, that intrepid voyager through the realm of
myth, noted that many of the world's great myths are founded
on a single theme, that of the circular journey to find and bring
back the treasure-beyond-all-price, which we might call the
Heroic Quest. Joseph Campbell calls this theme the mono-
myth.[3] As an archetypal structure, it contains key elements
that appear to a greater or lesser extent in the symbols of all
myths of this type, regardless of their cultural origins. These
key elements represent recognizable stages, milestones if you
like, upon the way. Depending on the myth, some keys are
emphasized above others, and not all of the 'journeying' myths

contain all of the keys, but in most of them the archetypal elements are discernible.

I have chosen to call this the Heroic Quest rather than the Hero's Journey, the title by which Joseph Campbell's mono-myth work is more usually known, as the journey is common, with differences, to both men and women, and in both cases is about individuation and wholeness.

The journey we are talking about is the evolution of con-sciousness, which is also the journey back to the Self (you will remember that we looked at the difference between ego and Self in Chapter 2), back to the divine spark at our still and unchanging Centre, that which is at the same time our unique essence, and that which joins us to everything else. It is a journey back to wholeness. It is also a movement away from a purely material, or reductionist, definition of 'reality' towards a more spiritual perspective.

Loosely speaking, from the viewpoint of archetypal psychol-ogy the first stage of the journey involves a movement towards individuation – that is, a movement away from the collective and its values and its conditioning, and towards one's own path, a singing of one's own song. One then moves through an integration and synthesis of one's inner opposites and un-acknowledged parts, including and especially the inner male (animus) for a woman and the inner female, or anima, for a man, towards wholeness. Alchemy teaches us that a complete synthesis, union, cannot take place until the individual compo-nents have first been clearly separated and defined. Alchemically speaking, a marriage, inner or outer, between undifferentiated substances or beings is necessarily transient, and the inner sacred marriage, as the outer, is given firm foundations only when it takes place between two clearly defined individuals each standing in their own circle. Thus is the reconciliation of opposites achieved, and with this, too, we are able to move beyond duality, transcending the differentiating function of the opposites involved. The final stage is to make the journey back to the collective as a whole person with our own unique gifts to offer. Not everyone hears, or heeds, the Call to Adventure and steps out into this journey. Of those who do, some don't return. The journey inward is as fraught with danger as any journey into outer space.

In this book I have included two journeys which I feel are clear examples of the Heroic Quest. They are as relevant today as when they were first recorded, one in the early years of the first millennium AD and the other in the early years of this millennium. Archetypally, Psyche's is a 'woman's' journey, and Perceval's a 'man's', although of course both myths speak to both sexes. I cannot do either of these great myths the justice they deserve; partly because I do not pretend to be an expert in myth analysis, and partly because a chapter is not sufficient space. I will attempt to outline the archetypal 'meanings' behind the significant events, and refer any interested reader to the authorities who have devoted whole works to these stories, as detailed in the Notes section. What I do hope to do is whet your appetite for stories, and give you the flavour of the enormous power held in these ancient archetypal images.

Although to some extent I have adapted Campbell's Hero's Journey model, much of my understanding of it is based on teaching from the Transpersonal Psychology Study Centre, to the directors of which I am grateful.

In each person's life some aspects of this journey will be more apparent or carry more weight than others, and each individual will have his or her own 'sticking-place'. (An exploration of your personal myth or myths, as outlined in Chapter 6, may help identify where, if you are stuck, it is likely to be.) On a minor level, many of us repeat this journey at different times in our lives in different circumstances with cycles of varying significance, intensity and importance. Others may only be able to identify one major call-to-adventure and return, a decisive once-and-for-all journey, perhaps taken at adolescence, perhaps at mid-life. It is also possible that several cycles run simultaneously in one's life in different areas. You may, for instance, be 'bringing home the treasure' in your career-life, and still be struggling on the threshold with a manipulative mother or a possessive father in your relationship-world.

It is possible, too, to get stuck in endless questing, where perhaps the life 'below the threshold' with its tests and dragons and excitement and potential holds more promise than the idea of returning with the treasure and 'settling down'. This is especially true of what Archetypal Psychology (see Marie-Louise von Franz and James Hillman) calls the *'puer aeternus'* (*'puella aeterna'*) people, 'the eternal youths', Peter Pan people who are putting-off the moment of having to be grown up, and for whom the journey is all-important. This is illustrated in the tales of some of the mediaeval knights, where life was not worth living if you actually got to possess the princess and had to give up doing battle with dragons and pining over your lute because of unrequited love, instead to pace the battlements or rock a cradle! Brian Patten, the Liverpool poet, expresses this perfectly in his poem, 'Tristan, waking in his wood, panics'.[4]

I'd like to spend a little more time looking at the image of the Eternal Youth, before we move on to look in more detail at the monomyth model. This figure represents quite an important archetype for the generation of us who were growing up in the 1960s and 1970s. The 'flower children' cult represented a rejection of the 'grown-up' world, which was seen as stifling and blind with its materialistic consumer values, its conservatism and its adherence to a *modus vivendi* based on a bureaucratic sexist hierarchy. At this time, too, gender issues came to the fore with a (perhaps necessarily) militant feminism, the more radical members of which at times clothed themselves vociferously in the male suits (metaphorically speaking), which they were simultaneously condemning. Shortly afterwards, the 'new man' appeared with his long hair, rather effeminate garb and gentle passive ways. In doing away with the old repressive order, the androgyne was born. (I am not using the term 'androgyne' here in the way that Jung uses the idea of the Divine Androgyne, one who is beyond duality. I am using it to mean one who has not yet moved through the differentiation of opposites necessary before the union spoken of in alchemy as the Great or Sacred Marriage.) The Peter Pan figure, male or female, is often very charming, and the androgyny is significant. The act of completing the journey, while putting you in touch with your inner opposite, then also reclaims you for your own sex (but this does not mean that you become the stereotyped 'macho' male, or submissive, simpering female. It means rather that you become more clearly yourself. The 1980s and 1990s have seen a movement back to the middle, where women, having connected with their masculine side, are freer to touch their femininity once more, and the New Man, become more gentle and receptive, is rediscovering his wild side, or as Robert Bly expresses it, his fierceness. In the best possible sociological scenario for the future, the stage is now set for a new order to emerge, a true partnership of equals.)

This perpetual adolescent figure often finds it difficult to complete the inner journey, just as he or she may find it difficult to sustain a long-term relationship. There is often an 'airy' quality to him or her, perhaps a touch of the trickster. Like Tristan, what interests him (or her), is not the flesh-and-blood here-and-now, but the realm of perpetual possibility, that magical kingdom that always lies just around the next corner, over the next hill. Icarus, too, in his obsession with flying higher and higher towards the sun (and risking his life in doing so – another characteristic is this urge to sail closer to the wind than is safe) is another good example. Because these people are stuck in the kingdom of tests and ordeals, they have not met and integrated their inner Other – although, of course, they are not alone in this. In this situation the likelihood is that the latter will possess them unconsciously, making them more subject than usual to moods, dissatisfactions, restlessness, Divine Discontent. Those parts of the unconscious that we do not recognize tend to hold us in their grip one way or another. The qualities, negative and positive, of this unrecognized inner Other will be projected 'out there' onto whomever seems to us to most nearly fit the mask that we unknowingly are holding out (this is also an element that we all experience to some degree when we fall in love. Robert Johnson in his book *The Psychology of Romantic Love* expounds this theory brilliantly). But these people are often also very gifted, highly creative and imaginative types, and society needs them. So they are double-edged people. Like Hermes, the cosmic messenger, (who, better known as Mercury, is also the planetary ruler of Gemini) they have the ability to 'fly between the worlds', and while they may be bringers of light, they also at some level refuse to step out of the shadows.

A French book by Jerome Peignot,[5] which I read several years ago, argues the case for the androgyne from the philosophical standpoint that the Fall, the expulsion from the Garden of Eden, was the point at which the primordial asexual figure split into two sexes, and our sorrows and our yearning on the earth-plane are due to our innate 'unremembered memory' of our origins. (Peignot goes on to argue that both love and language are products of the blood of the wound of the Fall). (We are of course all familiar with the idea of our lost 'other half', which in our society is seen as a real person in the outer world, and the search for whom is the apparent – and that word is important – *raison d'être* of the quest for romantic love, which in our culture has its origins in the mediaeval highly-stylized institution of courtly love.) But while the somewhat asexual adolescent androgyne, of course, holds the seeds of potential totality, as long as he or she stays in the underworld of quests, the cycle is not completed and the return is not made. The return is only effected by the movement through the stages of the Heroic Quest, so that acknowledgement of and union with our inner Other is a step towards reclaiming our own whole-ness, being a complete person while still fully claiming one's own gender. At this point transcendence of the duality is possi-ble. This means that the return is not made by a sexless being, but by one who fully embraces not only sexuality as union but also his or her own differentiated gender, while recognizing that this duality is a product of our perception of the earth-plane on which we live, and to that extent, Maya, illusion.

> It is necessary
> to do that which
> the inner journey dictates.
> To do otherwise
> is to fly
> into all the faces of adversity
> towards certain death
> without choice of transformation.
> It is necessary to submit.
>   Lizzie Spring[6]

And so, finally, to a closer look at the Heroic Quest (see Figure 14). In common with other traditions such as Buddhism and shamanism, this can be looked at as an eight-fold path. From this perspective, these are the archetypal stages:

1. THE CALL TO ADVENTURE

The Call is the call from our own Self. Most of us spend a large part of our lives living, as it were, on the perimeter – living in the concentric ripples on the surface of the pool, responding to every breeze, rather than at the true centre, but there comes a time when this is not enough, when we have moved too far away. It is not always easy to hear the voice from the centre, let alone heed it – our lives are usually too busy, too cluttered, even to let the voice in, let alone find space to re-arrange our

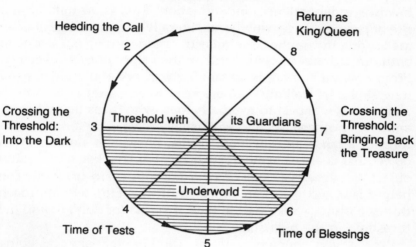

Figure 14

schedules to do something about it. Our own attachments keep us fixed here on the periphery – our fears, our hopes, our desires and addictions, our routines. More often than not, as I noted in the introduction, it will be an external crisis that forces us to stop and take notice, usually when it simply becomes too painful to carry on as we have been. I have already mentioned, in the context of the Wound, that there are particular times in our life when we are most likely to hear the call – for while the journey is unique to each person, some stages in life are more critical or more conducive than others.

In the myth of Psyche, the call to adventure comes when she starts her search for a husband, in the form of the pronouncement from the oracle that she is to go to her wedding, which will, she assumes, also be her doom.

2. HEEDING THE CALL

Responding to the call means taking the first steps on the path towards independence, individuation. This is an initiation, a rite of passage. In leaving home, literally or metaphorically, we are leaving the mother, the collective, and turning our backs on both our old way of being, and on the values of that collective. From now on, we are in unfamiliar territory and we will need new skills. In walking courageously towards these new horizons, we can expect to meet a helper, who takes many forms, animate or otherwise, and will usually have a gift for us, in the form of a talisman, question, riddle, answer or similar, or an object that is also a symbol, such as a box or a key or a natural object, or perhaps a cloak or sword or musical instrument. The helper is a god from our inner pantheon. How we approach this departure plays a part in how we cross (or don't cross!) the threshold in the next stage.

Psyche, you remember, despite thinking that she was going to her death (as she was, in a way) walked calmly and courageously to the high rock to meet her future.

3. THE THRESHOLD OF ADVENTURE

This is the big step into the unknown, off the rock. The threshold is guarded and there is usually a struggle. This is the night sea voyage and is a fearful time; one enters alone into the dark. Most societies have had, and some cultures still do have, this ritual of initiation, which is a death-and-rebirth. An offering needs to be made to the threshold guardian. Something is always given up (death to an old way of being), but something is gained, too (usually something previously held by the guardian). The guardians on the threshold are shadow-figures from one's own unconscious, animus or anima, possibly the mother or father, perhaps brothers or sisters. At this point there is no return; the journey has chosen you and there is no turning back, no way out. Once this is realized, one of two things happen – either fear claims you and you go under, or fear claims you, you meet it with courage and you win through. It may be that a confrontation with and movement through one's own fear is a necessary part of this stage. However, it is possible to see this journey into the dark as a chance to develop night-vision. Rather like the beheading image that I have already mentioned, it may require a different way of seeing before you are able to move forward, leaving behind the ordinary prosaic consciousness of everyday. The struggle on the threshold in myth sometimes results in physical death for the hero/ine. Death and rebirth. It would seem that a man may need to do battle in order to cross the threshold. For a woman, though, I suspect a 'letting go' is what gives her safe passage into the darkness of the Underworld, the realm of Soul.

Psyche, helped by her own courage, crosses the threshold. The threshold – limen – is an important place where a vast amount of energy is held. Passing over it we are now in the subliminal – below-the-threshold – world; the unconscious, the realm of Soul. Psyche is helped in her transition by the west wind (on the Medicine Wheel, west symbolizes water and therefore the emotions, introspection and solitude. It is also the place of death and rebirth, of transformation.) Psyche is reborn into a new way of life in the contentment of Eros' palace. Eros is invisible, and psychologically speaking, unconscious – he cannot bear Psyche to see him in the light of day. Psyche lives in the peace of blissful ignorance until her sisters, who are both reminders of the life she has left behind and components of her own unconscious, prompt her to challenge Eros to reveal his identity. Eros, as Psyche's animus, is immature. When Psyche challenges his male authority (for, as Robert Johnson notes in *She*,[7] she has started to feel imprisoned by the man she loves, as a woman is when her animus remains unconscious), and in effect drags him into the light (of consciousness), Eros gets angry and flees (back to his mother!) It is significant that Eros is a god. In this, her brush with divinity, we are given a clue to the nature of Psyche's journey. She is not ready, as yet, to deal with the awesome nature of this encounter with the numinous, and to this extent she, too, will now be wounded. We looked earlier in the book at the wound left by an adolescent encounter with the numinous; we shall meet it again in the tale of Perceval. This first union of Psyche and Eros is the 'false' or 'little marriage' of alchemy, where the two participants are not yet sufficiently separate and distinct as individuals ('individuated') to be able to come together in the binding union of two whole beings. However Psyche, in challenging her unconscious mate, has removed some of his power over her. But now the real work begins.

4. THE TESTS

At this point the traveller meets the ordeals that will severely test, temper and strengthen him or her. In many myths there are shape-shifting elements, which tell us of transformation, a shift in consciousness. Here we may meet our power-animals as well as our enemies. Part of the transformative process requires that we reclaim our instinctual nature, and part of it requires that we look at the world from different perspectives, become for at least a short while a different being. We can help this process by spending time consciously identifying with, *becoming*, for instance, an animal (or bird, or fish) whose skills we would like to learn, through whose eyes we would like to view the world. The tests may take the form of ordeals set by the four elements (e.g. 'death by water' and the like). There is usually a helper, perhaps as mentioned in the form of a friendly animal, or a wise person, or an apparently inanimate object, or our own positive inner animus or anima figure.

I see the four tasks of Psyche as particularly important metaphors for the inner work that is demanded on this journey.[8] To my mind they fall neatly into elemental tests, although it has to be said that it is possible to see more than one element at play in each group. This is my grouping:

(a) Sorting the Seeds: An Earth Task

This is to do with restoring order. It is about sifting through the elements of a confused situation in order to clarify; about learning classification, selectivity, discrimination, sorting that which is important from that which is obscuring it. It is part of the differentiating work I have mentioned above; the seeds heaped together can represent the raw muddled primordial mass of chaos: '. . . a rough, unordered mass of things . . . warring seeds of ill-matched elements heaped in one . . .' (Ovid, *Metamorphoses*). Psyche is aided by ants, symbols of structure and order, animals (or insects, rather) that live very close to the earth and that have a highly organized social system. They also represent the instinctual side of our nature. There is nothing grandiose or glamorous about ants, and there may be an important message here about the humbler and overlooked parts of our nature being the very aspects that will pull us through when we are stuck between the rock and the hard place. This repetitive type of task that engages our hands can also be the kind of meditative action that loosens the rest of our being into a different reality, like reciting a mantra or telling a rosary. Learning to stay with a muddled kind of situation that cannot be hurried until a different perspective becomes possible, or clarity emerges from the chaos, is an essential prerequisite of growth, perhaps especially for 'fire' people to whom patience does not come easily, and to whom repetitive tasks or routines are anathema. The seeds may also be important symbols of the potential for new growth. Clarissa Pinkola Estes in her book[9] quotes a Russian fairy tale that contains this same motif of sorting the seeds. Estes mentions theories that hallucinogens made from wheat, barley or poppy seeds were used in the old Eleusinian Goddess rites in Greece, and that this motif may be seen as a contacting also of one's powers for healing self and others. If the hallucinogenic angle has validity then this motif may also be symbolic of a preparation for a change of consciousness. Estes says that the heroine is being asked not only to 'separate this from that, to know the difference between things of like kind – such as real love from false love, or nourishing life from spoiled [or damaging] life' (my insert) – but also to be able to distinguish one medicine or drug from another.

(b) Bringing Back the Golden Fleece: a Fire Task

For a woman this is about reclaiming her own power, which many of us give away continually in our lives. There are two specific dangers in this test for a woman; one is that in emulating the traditional 'male' way of taking power, she may lose touch with her own more gentle nurturing aspect, and the other is that if she wanders in to the rams (and the rams with the golden fleece, sun-beasts, are fearsome indeed) innocent and unprepared, she might well be destroyed. She is warned against marching up to the beasts and battling for the fleece; she must use a different strategy. She is told to wait for sun-down. This is quite an important symbol. The twilight hour is one of those borderland times when anything might happen, the 'witching-hour' when the solar (male) energies are giving way to the lunar (female) energies, and there is an almost physical hiatus, as if the world stops to draw breath before changing direction. The fierce activity of daytime and its crea-tures is giving way to a settling down ready for the night; the sun and its followers are preparing for rest and so are less watchful, more subdued. Twilight also represents that hazy space that is neither consciousness nor unconsciousness but partakes of both. As a fire test it is also about creativity and imagination, both of which are useful in finding other ways besides the obvious of achieving your ends and bringing back the fleece. What I should also mention here is that at the point when the green reed spoke to Psyche, she was so much in the throes of despair that she was ready to kill herself. As often happens on the journey, it is at the point where you are ready to give up that the helper appears. (Robert Johnson, again in *She*,[10] comments: 'Almost always in human experience the urge towards suicide signals an edge of a new level of conscious-ness'.)

(c) Filling the Jar: An Air Task

In a way this is similar to the earth task in that it is about discrimination, but it is about the more usually 'masculine' attribute of focused concentration on detail, and specifically about learning perspective. The eagle (an air symbol, and mas-culine, so representative of the animus) represents the ability to step back to assess the overall picture from a distance before picking out relevant detail. That way one is not swamped by the icy waters that seem overwhelmingly threatening in the foreground, and it is possible to see from a distance what is not apparent close-up, the safe paths in a dangerous situation (the dragons). The river, of course, is the river Styx, and at some point in every journey there will be a time when a brush with death is inevitable. Learning how to fly above these situations and developing sharp sight and objectivity may help!

(d) The Descent to the Underworld: A Water Task

Psyche equates this with death. I see the first part of this final task as being about the honing of Psyche's emotional boundaries, especially with regard to being in touch with one's needs and feelings. It is also about developing will. (I shall treat the journey towards and across the Styx as the fourth task, and the entry into Hades itself as the Supreme Ordeal.) This fourth task may well be the most difficult of the four for many women in our culture. Water needs to be channelled, but for many of us setting our emotional boundaries is extremely difficult, especially so if you have dependents. In order to 'come out alive' it is crucial for women to learn how to say no, both to their own neediness and to that of others. It means to be prepared to push on regardless, no matter what distractions put themselves in your way, and no matter how many people request your help, if in heeding these things you will lose your own way in the darkness. It also means learning to be so fully in touch with your feelings that you also know when it is appropriate to instead say yes, for as with the task of collecting the golden fleece, getting the balance right is also important; being clear about your limits while still living compassionately and empathically. For many women, though, learning to put oneself first occasionally is the difficult bit.

Psyche's life depends on her ability to keep her objective in sight. This means that three times she has to refuse to respond to calls for help. In the terms of the myth, her actions, in the light of a culture bound by Christian ethos, could be labelled as selfish in the extreme, and many women have an enormous fear of being, or being seen to be, selfish. Both the maternal instinct and cultural conditioning conspire to make many women feel uncomfortable if they are not on hand to meet everyone's needs. Martyrdom draws higher praise. (I am not implying though that the path of service is not a valid path, provided one's motives are pure – that is that service comes from an open heart, not from merely a need to be needed. There is an American Indian story where the heroine wins through – and wins her prince – *as a direct result* of stopping on her own immensely important journey (which is a competition) in order to help others, despite her assumptions that this will lose her the one thing in the world that she wants above all others – the hand of the prince who will be given to the winner in marriage. Many European fairy tales incorporate this path too.) However, translated into less mythic terms, this part of the journey is about developing the kind of clarity, focus, strategy and single-mindedness that will enable you to sort and identify important objectives, and once you are clear about what these are, finding the courage and willpower to stay with them, within your own boundaries. This may mean a struggle with depression or inertia; staying with an unsatisfactory status quo is often an easier and tempting alternative to making the (often painful and lonely) changes that will bring you back up out of the underworld. In some ways this final task, then, is a synthesis and culmination of the previous three; developing will-power to use the wisdom already gained to take the final descent and come out alive.

5. THE SUPREME ORDEAL

This point is the final and major confrontation with death. Assuming that the hero or heroine has 'passed' all the tests to date, and that the powers that reside in the underworld have remained friendly, the reward for undergoing this ordeal is the treasure-beyond-all-price. In myth this is usually finding and marrying the prince or princess, the inner other, or a symbol that represents this. This of course is the Sacred Marriage of alchemy. If, however, the underworld powers have remained antagonistic, or the protagonist has behaved less than honourably, either death will take him or her, or he or she may decide to try and steal the reward that can only be rightfully gained through work and courage. He or she will then have to flee and be pursued, and eventually start the cycle all over again.

Just as one wouldn't run a marathon without appropriate training, so the journey back out of the underworld requires a strong ego. There is a common misapprehension among some Western devotees to Eastern spiritual systems that one is unable to be holy if one hasn't 'got rid of' one's ego. The ego has its place, and a healthy acquaintance with the ego and its strengths and weaknesses leaves one better equipped to know when its demands are appropriate and when not, when transcendence is possible and when not. A weak or fragile sense of self (ego-self) may mean that at this stage on the journey you wander lost and fragmented in the shadows.

Psyche, in following the instructions of the tower to the letter, manages her journey in and out of Hades smoothly, right up until the last moment, when her curiosity about the contents of the jar – which was not hers – and vanity (the desire to steal a little of the ointment to make herself as desirable as possible to Eros), in other words, her humanness, (not to mention her exhaustion) overcomes her and she opens the box, and thereupon falls down in a deadly swoon (and joins, briefly, the other mythic heroines, such as Snow White in her glass coffin, and Sleeping Beauty on her bed in the thorny thicket). This motif is common at this point in Hero's Journey myths; the hero or heroine is virtually home when the Underworld as it were reaches out to try and take the traveller captive one last time. Often the hero or heroine succumbs briefly once again to the world of the unconscious by falling asleep. At this point he or she seems to have one foot in the water and one on *terra firma* – a foot in each world. Sometimes the treasure is temporarily lost and further tests arise. However, it is as if there is an invisible threshold crossed; provided one foot is on dry land (and the time is right and the descent has been made with honour), from this point on the traveller is safe. So Psyche's ordeal is over, and Eros, seeing her plight, immediately flies to rescue her. She has found her treasure-beyond-all-price.

6. THE QUEST ACHIEVED

The union is blessed. At this point there is a reconciliation with the god or goddess – that is, after the Sacred Marriage with one's inner opposite, there is a reunion with one's own sex, a reclaiming of the power of the feminine or masculine. A personal healing occurs, and there is a euphoric sense of paradise regained. There is a wonderful prolonged banquet, much laughter and joy and singing. All is well in the Garden.

Psyche has married Eros, the union is blessed by all the gods and goddesses, and Psyche (maiden) and Venus (woman) have made their peace. An initiation has taken place.

7. THE RETURN TO THE THRESHOLD

Stage 6, the 'honeymoon time', claims as many victims as does the stage of tests. After the fear and the danger of the previous ordeals, who wouldn't want to linger in the Garden of Eden with their beloved? But a short honeymoon is all that's possible. This is after all still the Underworld, and the journey is not completed until the treasure has been brought back to the world. Once again, there is likely to be a struggle, again there is a meeting with the guardian, again something will need to be given up in order to return to one's everyday world and 'ordinary' consciousness. The hero has to turn his back on the timeless bliss of paradise, and be reborn back over the threshold, bearing the treasure – his or her own soul. This return, bearing your own unique gift to offer to the collective, has similarities with what Native Americans call making an Act of Power in the world.

8. RETURN TO THE WORLD AS KING OR QUEEN

The act of bringing back the treasure restores fertility to the Wasteland, causes the waters to flow again, heals the wounds. This offering of one's own wholeness to the Collective is the lighting of another candle towards universal healing.

The union of Psyche and Eros results in new life, in the birth of a divine child, Pleasure, also known as Bliss.

EXERCISE – A JOURNEY TO THE HEALING SPRING

Read the exercise through carefully to yourself once or twice until you can picture it. If you prefer to read it aloud into a tape-recorder to play it back to yourself, do so. Then, starting as always from your sacred space, close your eyes and take yourself as usual to your sanctuary.

It is early morning. Give yourself a minute to absorb the feel of this time of day in this place. When you are ready, ask for a vehicle. What comes to you could be anything – a horse, a car, a pair of wings, a motorbike, roller-skates, a dolphin, a canoe. Whatever your vehicle is, take careful note of it as it comes towards you. In it, (or on it) you are going to travel from your sanctuary to the sea-coast. (Remember you are in the Otherworld which has its own laws, so there is no need to worry about the practical aspects of, say, a journey overland with a dolphin!) Before you leave your sanctuary, remember to take with you the talisman that accompanies you on all these journeys.

On the way, you will pass through a dark forest; across an open windswept hilltop; you will ford a rushing river and cross through the middle of a high moorland plateau that is on fire around you. Eventually, though, you will come to a grassy clifftop, and the ocean is spread out before you. It is a gentle, balmy spring day, and the air is filled with the cries of seabirds and the scent of saltwater and sea-thrift. In front of you is a winding path which you follow down to the shingly shore at the foot of the cliff.

As you reach the bottom, you turn to look back at the clifftop high above you, and notice a spring of crystal-clear water fountaining out of the rock-face a few metres above the ground. You know that this spring has cleansing and restorative powers, and as you move towards it you see a flat stone just where the gushing water hits a small pool. Asking permission of the spirit of the spring, you sit or lie on this stone to be washed by the waters flowing from above. The waters seem to pour in and through every part of you, washing out all greyness, fear, anxiety, worry. While you rest there, you notice that although the spring is silver, the water in the pool at your feet glistens gold in the sunlight, and there are glowing stones and shells, and small bright fish darting around you. The peace and beauty and power of this place wash you completely clean of all your day-to-day concerns and restore a sense of balance and wholeness.

When you are ready to leave, you will need to make an offering of whatever seems appropriate – a special shell, a coin, a strand of your hair, a ribbon, a feather – which you place on the stone. If you look around you, you will also see a gift to you from the spring – this will be the first thing that you see after making your offering.

In a few moments it is time to leave this place. Thank the spring and its waters and journey back to your sanctuary by the easiest and quickest route. When you are ready, bring yourself back to your room and your body and everyday consciousness, returning slowly, stretching your limbs and wiggling your toes and fingers, finally opening your eyes.

Now record your journey in as much detail as you can, and if possible make a sketch of each of the important images from it, preferably in colour. Then ask yourself these questions:

1. How did I feel as I set out on my journey? (Fearful, excited, calm?)
2. What was my vehicle? (Describe it in detail.) Was I comfortable with it?
3. Did I have a 'helper' other than my vehicle?
4. How did I feel as I passed through each of the four 'danger spots'? (Close your eyes and recall them, then detail them one by one.)

5. Was there any one of them that I couldn't or didn't pass through?
6. Was there any particular obstacle that I needed to overcome? How did I overcome it? And if I didn't, how could I another time?
7. Is there anything I would choose to leave behind me another time?
8. Anything I would choose to take with me?

(NB: This visualization can be used to heal and strengthen on a regular basis. In this case omit the section that represents the four Ordeals by Fire, Earth, Air and Water, and also of course the questions.)

The Quest for the Holy Grail

There are many versions of and adjuncts to the story of the Grail. Many of these tales are very old – written down in the early years of this millennium, their origins are likely to be a great deal older than that. The Grail is still an important symbol for us, representing as it does humankind's striving towards the highest good, towards the light of consciousness and the promise, at some level, of everlasting life. The legends endure; generation after generation are entranced by them. The stories that make up the Grail material are basic teachings of a Mystery School, and as such portray a journey of initiation. Each of us undertakes the Quest in our own life-journey, if we have undertaken to approach this journey consciously. In the body of Grail material, many knights set out to search for the Grail, but only three, Galahad, Bors and Perceval, achieve it. Each of these three represents a different archetypal approach to the journey and experience of the Grail:

> For Galahad, the pure knight, is reserved the way of the Spirit, of direct communion with the godhead; for Perceval, the simple man . . . the way of dedication, of the Heart, which entails a long hard road towards self-realization; and for Bors, the ordinary man, who watches the events but stands a little apart from them, the way of contemplation, the Mind.[1]

I have chosen to follow the path of Perceval, the Holy Fool. I have based the story that follows on a synthesis of the versions of Chretien de Troyes, Wolfram von Eschenbach and the Welsh Peredur. Chretien's tale stops short before the second arrival at the Grail Castle, and I have combined one of the various Continuations by later authors with Wolfram's tale to complete it. Sadly, for the sake of space, the story that follows is very greatly abridged; I have retained the episodes that I want to look at in Chapter 8. As it is, each of the episodes or motifs requires its own chapter; I have not in any way been able to do the legend the justice it deserves.

*   *   *

There is serious trouble at the Grail Castle. A long time ago, the Fisher King, who reigns from the Castle, was severely wounded. For many years now he has been in great pain, constantly groaning and crying out; so much pain that he feels he cannot live, but he is unable to die either. Because a country reflects the nature and health of its king, the land around the Castle has become the Wasteland. The wells and springs have dried up, crops fail, children are sickly or stillborn, many of the women and animals are barren. The Fisher King, in his pain, has to be carried around in a litter. The only time there is any respite for him is when he is fishing. His only chance of healing will be when an innocent fool arrives at the court, and asks a specific question about the meaning of the Grail.

Each night there is a ritual procession at the Castle. Ceremoniously, three of the Grail Hallows are carried through by the Grail Maidens, headed by the only woman whom the Grail itself will permit to carry it, Repanse de Schoye.[2] There is a bleeding lance, or spear, a platter, and then the indescribably beautiful and luminous Grail itself. Each person present – with the exception of the wounded King, who is further punished by being forbidden to partake of the gifts of the Grail – is given wine from the Grail, which has the power to cure all ills and which brings all who drink from it their heart's desire.

Many miles away – and yet also close at hand – lives Perceval. Perceval has been brought up in a wild wood in the depths of Wales on his own by his mother. He is the third son. He is fatherless, his father and two brothers having been killed years before. Perceval has been brought up in a simple uneducated peasant sort of way, with little curiosity about or knowledge of the outer world (since he sees nothing of it.)

One day, the adolescent Perceval is hunting in the woods when three knights, dressed in all the trappings of knighthood, ride by. Perceval is so dazzled by these wonderful beings, that, after learning that they come from the court of King Arthur, he races home to tell his mother that he has met three 'angels', and that he is leaving immediately to join them – on his ancient bony piebald nag – at the court. His mother, desolate, begs and pleads with him not to go, and tells him that his father and brothers were all killed in knightly pursuits and she had attempted to save him from the same fate. Perceval completely ignores her anguish and simply reiterates that he is leaving, and asks her to put together some food. His mother has no choice but to let him go, with a homespun garment and some advice; if he passes a church (which she describes) to go in and pray; he should honour women and help those in distress; if he has the chance to obtain a ring from a maiden he should do so; and not to ask too many questions.

So Perceval sets out; innocent, clumsy, gauche and enthusiastic. He is, however, courageous, strong and swift. He looks back once, and catches a glimpse of his mother swooning on the bridge, but doesn't turn back. He asks everyone he meets about the three knights. At length he comes to a magnificent tent. Having only known his mother's rough hut, he assumes this must be one of the churches his mother talked about. He bursts in and sees a beautiful maiden sitting beside a banquet that she has prepared for her beloved knight, whom she is awaiting. Perceval in his innocence asks no questions, sits down to eat, and before leaving embraces the damsel and takes a ring from her finger as a keepsake, as his mother bade him. The maiden, accepting the intrusion as she recognizes that his intentions are innocent, tells him that he must make haste and leave before her knight, the Proud One, arrives and kills him.

Finally Perceval arrives at Arthur's court. He is the source of much amusement and ridicule for his garments, his mount and his naive requests to be knighted. Only a dwarf and his wife recognize Perceval for who he really is; his father was a great knight. They are beaten for their trouble. Arthur, however, receives him kindly and tells him that he has much to learn before he can be knighted. Next follow two important events for Perceval. One is that there is a maiden at King Arthur's court who has not laughed or smiled for many years. Legend in the court has it that the maiden will laugh when the best knight in the world appears, which she does as soon as she sees Perceval. Arthur knights him instantly, and Perceval challenges and overthrows many knights in his first week.

Soon after knighting, Perceval defeats, more by luck than judgement, the Red Knight, who has been insultingly rude and boorish to the court in general and the Queen in particular. No one to date has been able to subdue him. Perceval, who kills the Red Knight largely out of greed and covetousness for his fine suit of red armour, puts the latter on over his own rough garments. Perceval proceeds to ride off on the Red Knight's horse, and soon meets with a wise teacher, Gornemant, who

instructs him in the knightly arts. Gornemant also tells him that
he mustn't seduce or be seduced by fair maidens; he must
make every effort to find the Grail Castle; and that a knight
should learn by observing and listening, keep his own counsel
and not ask too many questions.

At this point, Perceval remembers his mother and thinks he
will ride off to see if she is all right; he remembers her swoon on
the bridge at his departure. However, before he manages to get
back to his mother he rescues Blanchefleur,[3] in distress in her
castle, who rewards him for fighting passionately on her behalf
with her love; the love between them, though passionate and
tender, however, is at this stage chaste, according to the ethics
of courtly love. She becomes his constant source of inspiration
and meaning, a companion of the heart and spirit even when
not physically present.

After a short rest with his lady at the castle of Belrepeire,
Perceval sets forth again, and comes to a deep river. He meets
with a fisherman, who directs him to the Grail Castle – which is
always close at hand – and it materializes in front of him as if
by magic. He just manages to cross the moat before the drawbridge clanks shut behind him, just touching his horse's heels.
The fisherman now reappears in the guise of the Fisher King,
and hands Perceval a rare and magnificent sword, courtesy of
the King's niece.

Perceval now witnesses the marvels and mysteries of the
Grail procession. He also catches a glimpse of the Grail King, a
beautiful, holy white-haired old man who is father to the
wounded Fisher King. He is so spiritual that all the food he requires is the Host offered from the Grail treasures. Perceval wants
to ask about all these mysteries, but doesn't; he remembers his
mother's words, and those of the hermit. He thinks he will ask a
servant in the morning. But when he wakes up the castle is totally
deserted, though his horse and armour are ready for him, and
once again he only just makes it across the drawbridge before it
clangs shut behind him and the castle vanishes.

Perceval continues on his way. He meets with a weeping
woman who is cradling the dead body of her knight. She tells
him that his mother died when he left, and she also reproaches
him for not having asked the question at the Grail Castle.
Soon after, he meets another sorely lamenting maiden in much
disarray, and recognizes her as the damsel from whom he took
the ring in the tent. She has been dreadfully punished by her

jealous knight, who also arrives, to be defeated by Perceval and sent, along with the girl, to Arthur's court. Arthur, on their arrival, sets out to search for Perceval, who by now has been long missing. By chance they pitch camp close by each other that night in a forest glade. When they awake the next morning, snow has fallen, and some of Arthur's knights come upon Perceval totally entranced by the sight of three drops of blood and a few black feathers in the snow, shed by a passing wild-fowl pursued by a hawk. He is suddenly reminded of Blanche-fleur, of her lips, her raven tresses, her milk-white skin, by the red blood and black feathers on the white snow, and is so enraptured that in his trance-like state he fights off two of Arthur's knights without even noticing. Then Gawain, who is noted for his fair words and gentle manner, approaches him and Perceval comes out of his trance and accompanies Gawain back to Arthur. On their return to Caerleon a feast is held in Perceval's honour.

In the middle of the festivities in rides the Loathly Lady, a totally abhorrent sight, the ugliest woman on earth. She proceeds to upbraid Perceval for his failure to ask the question in the Grail Castle. She adds to his guilt by reminding him that his failure in this quest will result in doom for everyone. She tells Perceval that he must find the Grail Castle a second time, and he swears that until he does he won't sleep in the same bed twice.

While Perceval is contemplating the meaning of the Grail, Gawain enters the story and has various adventures. Gawain has the task of seeking out the Lance while Perceval is seeking the Grail. Perceval now wanders about in a rather lost way doing deeds of knight-errantry but losing sight of the real purpose of the Quest. He is nearly consumed by the powers of darkness in the form of various demons and temptresses during this time. However, a lion befriends him, and a Wise One in a boat comes to his aid and offers him guidance. This period in his life lasts for several years. He is jolted awake one day, however, on meeting a band of courtly pilgrims on foot who reproach him for carrying arms on Good Friday. They are on their way to do penance with a hermit, and Perceval joins them, confesses his sins, and after being reminded yet again of his various faults and failings and advised to attend mass every day, is absolved. The hermit tells him that the Grail King is his (the hermit's) brother, the Fisher King the hermit's nephew, and Perceval's mother sister to both hermit and the Grail King, which makes Perceval cousin to the Fisher King and nephew to the hermit and the Grail King. (It seems from previous encounters that Perceval has had that most of the figures in the Grail legend are related to each other.)

The hermit then gives Perceval directions to find the Grail Castle a second time. As before, it is close at hand; just ahead and round the corner. Before he reaches the Grail Castle, however, he arrives at another castle, and on entering finds a black-and-white chessboard set up ready for a game. He seats himself and moves one of the pieces, and finds himself playing an invisible opponent, who checkmates him three times in succession. In fury, Perceval stands up to throw the board out of the window into the lake, but is reproached by a red-robed star-spangled water nymph who rises up out of the lake. Perceval nearly swoons with ecstasy at the sight of her. She sends him off on another adventure, in the course of which he meets and overcomes the Black Knight who rises from a tomb to fight him. He also overcomes a giant, and then after another river-crossing comes to Belrepeire, where there is a joyous reunion with Blanchefleur. She wants to marry him immediately, but he says he needs to complete his journey first. After several more magical, mysterious and dangerous encounters, including a safe crossing over a glass bridge, Perceval meets his sister, who leads him to the hermit, his uncle, who points him in the right direction once again.

Perceval arrives at the Grail Castle a second time, and once again the solemn procession presents itself. Perceval is older, wiser, less self-centred, and with years of tests, suffering, learning and experience behind him now. Finally the right man at the right time asks the right question. No sooner has he asked the question than the whole castle reverberates with the answer. Simultaneously with Perceval's question the Fisher King is healed of his wound, the parched land outside the castle walls bursts into a flowery paradise and the waters are free to flow again. The Wasteland is restored to fertility and beauty. This is not quite the end, however; Perceval has a fierce battle and then a reconciliation with a long-lost half-brother, Feirefitz, who we learn is pied, half black, half white. Feirefitz is then wed to the Grail Maiden, Repanse de Schoye, and Perceval is finally reunited with Blanchefleur. At this point, Perceval has now earned the right to be crowned himself as the new Grail King, and to claim his kingdom in wholeness.

8

Towards Wholeness – Healing the Wasteland

The Quest for the Grail is a story as much for our time as for any other time. There are many ways of interpreting it, but for our purposes it is about the journey from unconsciousness to consciousness. This carries within it the search for meaning and the Divine, the reconciliation with our inner opposite and the healing of our fragmentations, the movement beyond ego to the still centre, the Self; it is also about reconnecting specifically with the feminine principle and the restoring of the feminine, of Soul, to the world (though in the joining of the light of Spirit and the vessel of Soul as symbolized by the radiant luminosity of the Grail, these apparent opposites are transcended.) It is about, too, the reconciliation and merging of our inner and outer worlds. It tells us, also, how a simple action, performed in the right way at the right time, brings about the freeing of the waters. Though the journey may take a lifetime – or longer – of almost superhuman dedication and commitment, the right action couldn't be closer at hand. It is always there, just around a corner, waiting to be found by those whose 'doors of perception have been cleansed'.[1] It only requires opening our eyes and opening our hearts to the truth; being prepared to be fully human (in which I include being in touch, too, with our divinity), for the question is as simple as this.

The Grail itself as a symbol is extremely archaic and complex. There is a connection with the Celtic Cauldron of plenty, and of death and rebirth, transformation. In Christian terms it is of course connected with the chalice of redemption. It is the vessel for the highest good, and for all that is immortal. It embodies freedom, truth, compassion, beauty and never-ending abundance;

the place of the heart's desire and the heart's rest. As a feminine symbol it is also of course about fecundity; as a symbol for the Earth it is the vessel for Anima Mundi, the world-soul. It is also something different for each of us.

I want to emphasize, too, that while the Quest is a solitary journey, it is made for the good of the collective as much as for that of the individual. As I said in the Introduction, the transpersonal aspect of all of these teachings includes the idea of lighting a candle for the good of the whole. So the blessings of the Grail are for all beings.

The three tales on which I have based my telling, while sharing archetypal motifs, are each very different in emphasis. Each has its own nature and its own power, and in blending elements from each I have run the risk of diluting this. Peredur has contributed less than the other two. Peredur seems to belong to a much older order, and while still following the journey to maturity of an uncultured simple adolescent (in this case a seventh, rather than a third, son; either, in fairy stories, is gifted with unusual or magical powers, or destined for glory) brought up in forest seclusion, the storyline is vivid, complex, full of much slaying and also of many Celtic Otherworld motifs such as the green-and-burning-bush and the black sheep who become white on crossing the river, and vice versa. However, Peredur's journey has nothing to do with the Grail as a physical vessel, although there is a procession with a bleeding lance and a salver bearing a severed head. The main motivation of the story is how Peredur, through courage (and his courage is one of the most important aspects of all three tales), avenges – hundredfold – the death of a kinsman. We could say that Peredur's way is the way of Power.

Chretien's Perceval, written at the end of the twelfth century, is very much a child of its time. Many of the motifs, such as the four Grail treasures, or Hallows, have become Christianized, and though it is a tale of a spiritual quest it is written in the style of a courtly romance, heavily sprinkled with chivalric deeds, enemy knights, demons, dragons and evil temptresses to be overcome, beautiful if faceless ladies who, as the embodiment of perfection-to-be-worshipped-from-afar, provide inspiration and favours, and in the spirit of the time, the tale is founded on the concept of honour. Like Parsifal, it is about the quest for meaning, and we could say that its main motivation is truth, spiritual truth. The question in Perceval is subtly differ-

ent from the question asked in Parsifal, and in Chretien's version we are also given an answer. (We will look at these later
on.) An interesting detail: T. W. Rolleston[2] tells us that in
Cornish and Welsh the prefix 'per' means bowl or vessel,
directly connecting our hero with the Grail.

Wolfram's Parsifal is roughly contemporary with Chretien's
work; slightly later, it is a retelling in a different way, with a, to
me, more complete ending than Chretien's continuator's ending (or the continuator with whom I am familiar, anyway.)
Wolfram approaches his work with humour and compassion,
and the hero reflects this in his humanity. As in Perceval the
Grail is earned the hard way (significantly, the wounded Fisher
King inherited the Grail Castle, he didn't earn the right to be
there); and whereas Perceval achieves his enlightenment
through understanding the nature of spiritual truth, we could
say that Parsifal reaches his crowning by the path of love, compassion. Since the Grail Quest is a journey towards wholeness,
Perceval/Parsifal's path leads through a union of opposites and
the healing of inner fragmentations, from unconsciousness to
consciousness, from ego-oriented living to living from the Self.
At this point he is ready to give back to the community that
which will help restore the waters and make the Wastelands
blossom.

The Grail legends can be read at many different levels. I want
to reiterate here that, as part of a corpus of material related to
wisdom teachings, this journey is first and foremost an *inner
journey*; it has great impact when we realize that all the characters and all the encounters are aspects of our own inner world
and its dramas; the journeys, experiences and joys and de-
spairs common to all human beings, though, of course, the
form they take will differ, as will our awareness of them. The
King, the ruling masculine principle in the (Western) psyche, is
wounded; perhaps because of his lop-sidedness. If we look at
him as representing the Superior Function in Jungian terminology, it is especially interesting to hear that in one version of the
story at least his wound was self-inflicted with his own sword.
Too much air; too much Logos, too much rationality and too
little feeling, too little soul. His redemption comes from the
Fool; the underdeveloped clumsy untutored unconscious 'Inferior Function' part of himself, the childlike adolescent. The
women he meets are mostly anima-figures; the hermit and the
Grail King aspects of his psyche, too, as are the Red Knight and

the Black Knight, and all the other beings in the story. Emma Jung[3] points out that Perceval himself is an archetype; his development should not be understood only as an example of the movement towards consciousness of one individual, but also 'as a symbolic representation of a collective evolution'.

Jungian theory, as distinct from say Freudian or Kleinian theory, assumes two things that are relevant to the way I want to look at this quest. The first is, as I have said already, that whether we are conscious of it or not, we are motivated at a deep level by a search for wholeness; the second is that our psychological structure includes an innate 'religious' function; that is, a need for meaning. The Fisher King is wounded – that is, he is not whole – and the country around him is a wasteland, devoid of fertility. There are various different versions of how the King received his wound; in some it was an invisible (=Shadow) opponent; in some a pagan (also Shadow) knight; in some it was the stealing of a piece of red-hot (no pun intended!) salmon (that is, an untimely glimpse of wisdom/ knowledge for which he was not yet prepared – the Wound left by the first numinous experience of the adolescent, already discussed.) In another version it was a self-inflicted wound, a punishment for carnality. What is deeply significant is that the wound is in the genitals (often expressed as 'thighs'.)

For a man to be wounded in this way, in the genitals, in myth means many things. It means that his ability to relate is impaired; his generative/reproductive/creative functions are injured. He is severed from his feeling-function and his instinctual nature; he is sterile. Because a country reflects the state of its people and especially its king, his country has become a barren wasteland – this is true of both the inner and the outer landscapes. The Wasteland too is a symbol of a spiritual disorder; of the schism between church (spirit) and nature (soul); and, more relevant to our century, the split between materialistic consumerism and its exploitative reductionist approach to the universe, and an approach that respects the Earth and its wisdom, appreciates awe and mystery and makes space for mystical ecstatic experience. What has been lost is the feminine principle in both king and country; both soul and fecundity. One story tells us that the wells dried up after the well-maidens – the old Celtic goddesses of the waters – had been raped; not by the Fisher King but as a reflection of the state of things. Then, as in our century (and it is interesting that the older

Celtic tale of Peredur does not say quite the same thing about the Wasteland) the male principle of Logos ruled the land and feminine issues to do with love, compassion, creativity and fertility had been suppressed. According to Emma Jung:

> If a man becomes identified in an unbalanced way with his intellect and the fictions of his ego, he loses his relation to the anima, for which reason the unconscious torments him with emotions, irritations, lack of self-control, moods and depressions . . . [he may become] ruthless, arrogant and tyrannical.[4]

Much of our sense of meaning comes, according to Dr Jung, from a sense of connectedness with the realm of the unconscious, the realm of the feminine soul, and its mythic realities. (It could be argued that meaning also comes through our interpersonal relationships; while this is undoubtedly also true, for many people they are not, in themselves, enough, unless we ask them to carry far more of our needs than they can be expected to bear – of which more later. Besides, until we have made a creative fruitful relationship with ourselves and our psychic roots, we are unlikely to be able to make meaningful connections with others.) Ultimately the way forward needs to be a synthesis of these opposites; a new world-view based on and/and rather than either/or.

The only time the king feels any relief from his wound is when he is fishing, we are told. Fish represent unconscious content; so relief comes in the form of images (in dreams, visions or through active seeking) from the unconscious. *When the King is engaged in the work of making the unconscious conscious – bringing light to the dark places – he feels some relief.* Because there is a connection between fish and initiation, we are told something about the kind of journey that needs to be taken.

There is a ritual procession each night at the Grail Castle, in which, in our story, three of the four Hallows are carried through. These, as discussed earlier, are archetypal symbols for the quaternity of fire, earth, air and water (or in Jungian terms, intuition, sensation, intellect and emotion.) In Chretien these have become Christianized.[5] It is significant that four is the number of wholeness, and in Chretien's version only three Hallows are carried through. The sword is not part of the procession – it resides in the wounded king. The king's niece is to hand a rare and beautiful sword to Perceval when he arrives at the Castle; because of the involvement of the feminine here this sword will have been tempered by qualities such as compassion and mercy. As a symbol of masculinity, it is also important that it is an aspect of the anima which presents it to Perceval.

We now meet our Fool. Perceval leaves the mother, the collective, and crosses the bridge. Bridges are important places, thresholds, places of transition with much energy of their own. Perceval makes the transition from one world, one state of being, to another. His mother does not. She faints on the bridge and we learn later that she dies on it. Psychoanalysis would say that something of our mother-complex, our mother-attachment, must die in order for us to be free to move on into our own journey – even if, for a while, we carry our homespun garments with us. We learn that he leaves on a piebald nag – the black and white motif crops up several times and has various meanings; one is that he has one foot in this world and one in the Otherworld, and similarly that conscious and unconscious realms are mixed. Black-and-white represent the polarities, too, within our own nature as well as in the outer world. It is significant that at the end of the story we learn of Perceval's long-lost black-and-white half-brother, Feirefitz; in their reconciliation Perceval has embraced the opposites within himself and moved beyond them to a state of completeness, as symbolized by the two marriages – a quaternity being, as I have said, the number of wholeness.

Soon after leaving home, Perceval meets the first of many damsels. Like most of the other maidens she is an aspect of his anima, and his first encounter with her is rough and uncultured, ignorant; not surprisingly, since he has been so sheltered. Basically, he takes what he needs, and leaves. Whether the damsel is an inner anima-figure or an outer flesh-and-blood woman, the effect of this kind of encounter is damaging. In the case of the damsel in question, we later meet her in deep distress as a result of being punished by her jealous knight, the Proud One, because of Perceval's unthinkingly selfish behaviour. It is no coincidence that it is Pride (or arrogance) that Perceval has to overthrow; he meets and challenges most if not all of the seven deadly sins in the course of his journey, and puts them in the service of King Arthur, the ego.

Since Perceval, in the course of his journeying, is to meet many damsels, we will look in more depth at this image. We know that, no matter what our physiological gender, none of us is wholly male or wholly female. Each of us has an inner opposite; for a man it is the anima, for a woman the animus, according to Jung. Without this contrasexual part, this seed of the opposite within us, relating to someone of the opposite sex would be a virtual impossibility, so far away from each other we would be psychologically as to feel like a totally different species (*all* the time, rather than just some of it!) A hypothetical partnership in this case would mean that the two partners would be so polarized in their orientation that no sharing of any roles would be possible, and each would be unable to survive, quite literally, without the other. We talk of opposites attracting; but unless there is *some* underlying common ground on which to meet, this kind of magnetic attraction is usually followed by an equally strong repulsion. It would be a case, too, of the blind leading the blind; a model I use in my work-shops to illustrate this is shown overleaf (see Figure 15). The second model is the familiar Oriental symbol of wholeness; it is through our contrasexual 'eye' that we are able to perceive and have some understanding of our partner, and progress ourselves through a reconciliation of our opposing parts, trans-cending duality. We would otherwise be fixed, static. It is the anima or animus that is the guide to this other world.

Unlike many other world cultures, our European culture, which has its roots in the mediaeval troubadour tradition of courtly love, founds marriage on the concept of romantic love – initially blissful but ultimately shaky ground as regards long-term hopes. For many of us, in a culture and epoch that offers very little in the way of ecstatic, mystical or spiritual experi-ence, often our only contact with the transcendent realm comes through the experience of that bliss and passion that constitute falling in love. It is often the only place we have to put our unmet needs for union, for a sense of divinity. Because of this, there is a cultural addiction to romantic love and a confusion, too, of erotic ecstasy with spiritual liberation.[6] There may be a connection, but they are not synonymous; and the confusion between the two leads to much unhappiness. Our beloved is expected to carry the full weight of all our unmet needs and longings; not just the emotional ones, but the unarticulated needs for transcendence and union too. In addition to this, if we are still young, immature, or stuck in the land of quests and tests, like the *puer aeternus*, or just prone to falling in love, our beloved will not be perceived as the real man or woman he or

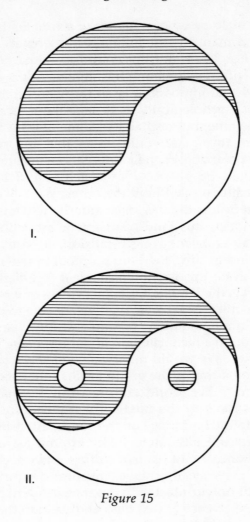

Figure 15

she actually is, but will be seen largely through the lens of our own projection; that is, we will be falling in love with our own anima or animus, projected onto whomever it fits with the least distortion. I am not saying that there is anything wrong with romantic love; it is a wonderful experience, one of the few human experiences that gives us a sense of vastness and awe and, for a time at least, ego-less bliss. What I am saying is that what causes unhappiness is expecting romantic love to carry more than it can or should bear; expecting our partner to make us eternally happy, expecting our soul-yearnings to be met once and for all. Romantic love in terms of human relationships is at its best the prelude, the doorway into a lasting love that consists of truly seeing and loving our partner for what he or she is, an ability to offer that person unconditional love, compassion and openheartedness, and wanting the very best for him or her because they are who they are.

This kind of maturity in our love-relationships is difficult until we have acknowledged our inner Other; until we can disentangle our image of the perfect man or perfect woman, or our own anima or animus, from our outer partners. When we have managed this, even if we cannot articulate it, (and it won't always be conscious) we free ourselves and our partners to be who we/they are as we reclaim our projections. In so doing, we also liberate an enormous amount of psychic energy as we no longer look to our partner to compensate for our deficiencies. We can then relate as two whole people, rather than two halves.

Returning to our story, Perceval meets many damsels, or aspects of his anima, but it takes him a while before he learns how to relate to them. Until he himself has become more individuated, more differentiated, more truly himself, the damsels also remain undifferentiated, faceless. Because he is young and egocentric he is careless about his treatment of them. He is not yet ready for the Great Marriage; much more tempering of his sword is needed, more compassion, and a greater degree of maturity with its sense of self and other and then the ability to transcend these distinctions in union and intimacy. A person ready to make the Great Marriage, the blessing of wholeness, is both a clearly defined individual, and someone who knows about relating. The first is the gift of the masculine, the latter the gift of the feminine. Perceval is still learning the tools of masculinity; he is too interested as yet in wielding his new-found sword and seeking adventure to be open to the lessons of the feminine. The Fisher King is too entrenched in his patriarchal position to soften to the feminine; Perceval has not yet sufficiently left the unconscious pull of the feminine (the mother) to be able to look upon it 'whole and against a wide sky'.[7]

While on the subject of damsels, a very brief look at the damsel who hadn't laughed for several years. Perceval may not as yet be conscious of it, but by his very arrival at the court of King Arthur he has at some level touched the feminine, acknowledged her; whereupon the spell is broken and she is free to smile and laugh. At this point, interestingly enough, our hero is taken seriously by the other knights and the king.

Perceval soon meets his first test as a knight in the form of the Red Knight, who, as a shadow-function, represents the rude, impetuous, aggressive mars-type energy of raw masculinity; a mediaeval prototype of a football hooligan. As Perceval is rather rude and boorish himself, and, what's more, covets the Red Knight's armour, he meets fire with fire and kills him without further ado. In doing so, and donning the red armour (though he needs some help to work out how to get it off the dead knight!), he takes on this unchannelled rather savage male energy for himself, though not without a struggle; that is, he disempowers the Red Knight (in a terminal way!) in order to empower himself; rather like the hunter who chains a pair of buffalo horns to his car-bonnet, or mounts a lion's head on the wall. (Symbols of power in our society at the present time tend to be symbols of wealth; so the youth who steals badges off Mercedes cars, or BMWs, or cars themselves, is at this stage of development; not as yet very conscious of what it is he wants, other than the fact that someone else has got it.) What Perceval has done symbolically is to access this energy consciously, to transfer it from the unconscious to the ego. Later he will learn how to subdue and channel this energy as appropriate, without having to smash it to pieces in the taking; more like schooling a wild horse. In Peredur, the hero kills endlessly and apparently indiscriminately; in Perceval/Parsifal the hero tends after this first killing to send all his conquered but living victims back to pledge themselves to Arthur; a subtle shift in evolution of the archetype in the intervening time between the tales.

Having also taken over the Red Knight's horse (that is, instinctual energy), Perceval rides off, and meets a wise teacher and father-figure, Gornemant (remember that Perceval was fatherless). Role models of their own sex are crucial for adolescents. Robert Bly suggests that, because of the way our society is, there are many wild (savage) 'unfathered' men running around rather frantically at the moment. As a woman I hesitate to comment any further on this; but would also say that many of the role models (politicians, movie-stars and so on) leave a little to be desired in terms of the wisdom and compassion they offer and respect they command; a reflection of society's values, or lack of them, as much as any individual's own contributions, as well as mirroring the confusion in the world as a whole.

Perceval now remembers his mother, and rides off to find her. On the way, though, he meets and rescues Blanchefleur, and they exchange love. This contact is more personal and intimate than his previous encounters with women; she is given a name, ('Blanchefleur', or 'white flower', like white dove, is a synonym for the soul) and although Perceval is not yet ready truly to relate to an external woman and establish a real relationship, she becomes important to him, and when he rides off, in a metaphorical way she travels with him, despite the fact that they will not see each other again for a long time. This meeting is an important symbol for Perceval's own inner development, representing as it does the Lesser Marriage we spoke about in the last chapter.

It is shortly after this that Perceval arrives at the Grail Castle for the first time. The Grail Castle – as with the Otherworld – is always close at hand and always here and now; just requiring the right eyes, right heart, right intention, as we have said. It keeps its own laws – 'Here Space and Time are One'.[8]

Four things happen here; Perceval is handed a sword by the King's niece, a relative of Perceval himself, we learn later; he witnesses the Grail Procession in the presence of the Fisher King; he catches his first glimpse of the saintly Grail King, a white-haired old man who is so spiritual that he only needs the nourishment of the Host from the Grail each day. He is a symbol of Perceval's own Self, and is that contact with the numinous we have already spoken of, a glimpse of the realm too powerful for an adolescent to bear it for long (the ego will not yet be strong enough), but the force of which acts like a thorn in the flesh, prodding the traveller into perpetual searching until he finds it again. There is a reflection here of the Fisher King's wound; from now on a sense of being in exile will creep into the hero. The fourth thing that happens is Perceval's failure to ask the question; he is not yet ready to 'stop the world'.

Riding away from the Grail Castle Perceval starts to encounter evidence of the suffering he has caused through his earlier thoughtlessness, in the form of various distressed damsels, and the news of his mother's death. As he becomes aware of the consequences of his actions so his own grief and guilt increase. While Galahad achieves the Grail through the purity of his lifestyle, Perceval struggles time and again with his weaknesses, and it is this continuing struggle and the humanness and compassion that arise out of this that in the end bring him his salvation. Emma Jung[9] points out that as we grow in consciousness so simultaneously, at least to begin with, our sense of guilt grows. In our story the sin is a sin of omission, or ignorance *of our own* unconsciousness; a sin against the feminine, the soul, and in our own century this still applies; most of the well-maidens are still missing, and in the words of James Hillman 'because of our neglect, the world is strewn with unrelated objects'; for it is the connection with soul, with the imaginal world of the unconscious, that restores relationship and meaning.

It is the drops of blood in the snow that prompt Perceval into setting off to make amends to one of the suffering women, Blanchefleur, who has had to endure Perceval's continued absence and neglect. There is much symbolism in this passage; the obvious connection of blood with suffering; the alchemical motif of the union of the red man with the white woman; and Emma Jung notes too the hawk as a symbol of the predatory aspect of the man in love, and the duck as bride/prey. Blood in fairy stories is also often a clue or a pointer to the path to take.[10] Perceval is thrown into a deep trance as he contemplates these things and is reminded of his beloved and aware of his wish to be reunited with her. First, however, he is reunited with Arthur and his knights. Significantly, it is the gentle Gawain who successfully breaks Perceval's trance; Gawain, whose task is to seek out the Lance rather than the Grail, embodies something of the feminine.

Perceval's next encounter is with the Loathly Lady, a dark aspect of his anima, who also heaps guilt upon him and reminds him of his duty to the Grail Castle. Like other aspects of his anima she is an agent of transformation, a guide to consciousness and individuation, and must be acknowledged; Perceval has to learn to accept both the dark times and the dark in his own nature.

An inevitable part of the journey towards consciousness is a wilderness time, the 'dark night of the soul' or the 'night-sea voyage'. At this point in one's life there is a sense of being lost and despairing; it is always 3 am and you are always on your own. Perceval spends some years lost in the wilderness, forgetful of the purpose of his quest, wandering rather aimlessly. In modern psychology this is known as the mid-life crisis, and can occur any time between thirty-five-ish and forty-five or so. It might last a matter of weeks or it might last years. It is a forceful pull from the soul, a turning inwards – Jung says that there is a movement from extroversion towards introversion in the second half of one's life; this tug needs to be attended to and accepted rather than resisted; when the metamorphosis occurs, when you come through, you will be speaking with your own voice, singing your own song. There are temptations and tests to be met; it is all too easy to drown the inner voices in frenetic outward running away; in new relationships, the latest techno-logical gadgetry, fast cars, more holidays, in excess drink or drugs or sex or parties or trying to recapture the promise of adolescence. Light relief is all right; permanent escape is unhelpful. Perceval meets his own demons and seductive temptresses; his own instinctual/solar nature (the lion) and the wisdom of the sea-borne part of himself help see him through, though he comes so close to being consumed by the powers of darkness that in his self-disgust and anger he wounds himself with his own sword, thereby strengthening the link with the Fisher King part of his nature.

Perceval is finally jolted out of this lost time by the hermit – the introverted wise part of himself; the one who can shine a light on what we need for our wholeness and where we need to look. The wisdom of the hermit-archetype is the gift of this dark time. To go willingly, as I have said before, lessens the risk of your unconscious immobilizing you in order to force you to pay attention through apparently external events such as divorce, redundancy, accidents or sickness. The hermit tells Perceval that they are of the same family – that is he is part of Perceval – and reminds him yet again how close at hand the Grail Castle is.

Before he arrives though he enters another castle where he is checkmated several times by the mysterious invisible chess opponent; the triumph of the irrational and inexplicable over the known and rational. The red-robed water-nymph is import-ant. She is fully clothed (which we wouldn't expect since she rises out of the water), so complete and unequivocal, and the red of her robes represents passion and feeling, the instinctual feminine nature, and the stars on her robe connect her with divinity, hint at cosmic origins. Perceval is deeply affected by her; it is as if for the first time he allows his feeling-nature to really move him. Her red dress symbolizes the energy, passion and presence that is beginning to flow from the shadow into the feeling aspect of Perceval's nature. Perceval, significantly, lifts her out of the water; he brings her up from the unconscious into his accustomed world, where he lets her direct the next stage of his journey.

The Black Knight is the polar opposite of Perceval. He is a captive in the Underworld, imprisoned by the feminine, overwhelmed by feeling. The battle then is another internal battle between the opposing forces of consciousness and unconsciousness, between Logos and Eros, the world of reason versus the world of the instinctual. Momentarily Perceval is in danger of being swallowed up, consumed by the unconscious world of feelings, which in its own way is just as dangerous as remaining in the world of the intellect. (This part of the journey, nearly at the end but not quite out of danger, echoes Psyche's sleep after opening the box; a last attempt by the Underworld to hold you down.) He defeats the Black Knight and just to be sure also overcomes a giant, thereby saving himself twice from being overwhelmed by emotion. The red-robed figure who opened this door is also leading him to a place beyond these opposites, and in making the river-crossing to Belrepeire and the joyful reunion with his beloved, Perceval has made an important transition. Blanchefleur, overjoyed to see her paramour once again, wants their wedding to take place immediately. Perceval, however, knows that he needs to complete his journey by finding the Grail Castle once again and healing the maimed king. He leaves once more, promising to return as soon as he can.

There are several more mysterious and testing encounters and incidents, one of which involves a crossing over a magical moving glass bridge, which Perceval negotiates successfully; a final safe transition into the Otherworld and a higher stage of evolution. Perceval then meets his sister who leads him to the hermit. Once again Perceval is pointed in the right direction, and once again and almost immediately the Grail Castle appears before him.

Perceval is now very different from the innocent, foolish and self-conscious youth who first arrived at the Grail Castle. He is wiser and more compassionate; he knows that his own authority is valid; he need no longer follow the social mores that dictated his behaviour in the past and made him hold his tongue at the first visit rather than asking the all-important question. As he witnesses the Grail procession once again, the right man at the right time, he knows what the healing question is, and asks it.

The motif of the question is a common symbol in fairy-stories. It is usually the key into a different realm and almost always brings healing and release in its wake. The question is usually to do with truth or love. In our story it is to do with both. There are two questions, and as they are both important I have included both; and/and rather/than either/or. Chretien's continuator has the question thus: 'Whom does the Grail serve?' And in this questioning of meaning, purpose, truth, the Wasteland is healed. In this version, too, we have the answer: 'The Grail serves the Grail King!' (As distinct from the wounded Fisher King.) That is, the Grail is in the service of the trans-personal centre, the Self or Higher Self, the greater good; that which is larger than our personal ego and that links us with the rest of the universe; the godhead, the divine. Through his trials and his own efforts Perceval's focus has shifted. He no longer sees himself as the centre of the universe; he no longer relates to all experience from the standpoint of egoic needs and desires and fears. He recognizes that that which is immortal in him is inseparable from all that is, and that which gives meaning to his life is serving that greater purpose. This is the way of truth.

Wolfram's ending is subtly different and yet the same. The question here is a question of love, compassion. For the same reasons as above, Perceval's concern is no longer with his own happiness. His motivation for finding the castle once more is compassion for the wounded man, and his question is 'What ails thee, o King?' No answer is necessary; the asking of the question *is* the answer. In the tradition of Christ or Buddha, his own suffering counts for nothing, is offered as a sacrifice in the service of the healing of all suffering. In letting compassion dictate his actions, in letting go of the need to direct all experi-ence towards the fulfilment of his own personal happiness, thus enabling the healing of the Wasteland and the freeing of the waters, paradoxically he has also found his heart's desire.

EXERCISE: THE CUP AND THE SWORD: THE MASCULINE AND FEMININE WITHIN

Take yourself in your mind's eye to your sanctuary (you can if you prefer imagine yourself in some other place that is known to you, in which you feel safe and at home), and spend some minutes as usual preparing yourself; letting go of your day-to-day 'stuff', breathing deeply and opening yourself to the Otherworld. You have as always with this work your talisman with you.

This is your own journey, your own Quest, and in this one your inner knowing will guide you without my directions, other than to start you off. When you open your eyes in your sanctuary you will be aware that there are two paths leading away from you. One will lead towards water, and the other up the side of a hill or a mountain. You will choose to follow one of them initially as you go in search of your Cup and your Sword. You may find both objects in the same place, or you may find one and have to come back to take the other path for the second object. You may find one immediately; it is just as likely that one or both are quite difficult to find. Be prepared, as always, for surprises. Take your talisman with you, and ask for guidance – from it, from any beings you encounter or from your own Higher Self – as you go. Thank any being who gives you information. When you arrive at your destination, that is when you find the object(s) of your Quest, ask the object itself to guide you as to your next steps; is there a ritual you need to perform with Cup or Sword; should you leave it where you found it or move it somewhere else, or should it come back with you? Pay careful attention to any answers you receive, and to your own feelings in the presence of these objects. Take as long as you need, and come back when you feel you have completed your journey.

As always, record your work in detail when you come back. You will have a fairly clear picture of your own masculine and feminine natures from this journey, and also guidance on what further work needs to be done. Some people find with this exercise that they are also given guidance towards the union of these inner opposites, or spontaneously during the Quest find themselves performing a marriage ceremony of some kind.

Whatever comes to you, may it bring you something of your heart's desire; and all that remains for me to say is may my love go with you on your path, may blessings surround you, may you always live with an open heart, and may flowers blossom where you walk!

Child of heaven and earth
child of the starry splendours
may you be
rooted as a tree
free as a bird
joyful as the singing waters
and bright as the rising sun.

Epilogue

Whatever you can do or dream you can, begin it.
Boldness has genius, power and magic in it.

Goethe, *Faust*

WHERE NOW?

I'd like to close this book with a few words in summary. The mythic process, like anything else, is organic; growing and changing, expanding and contracting. I am not exactly the same person at the end of writing this book as I was at the beginning; in the process of writing I feel myself changing; new ideas arrive all the time, new insights and clarity have come out of the writing process. As always, I am aware that I am passing on what I am needing to work on and learn from in my own life. As a result of the creative and organizational processes involved in preparing a manuscript, and of the huge enjoyment I have had in doing so, I feel as if I am on the brink of new directions in my own life; I am constantly finding new myths, new ways of working with myth, new meanings in the 'old' myths. The writing of this book, in fits and starts, has taken me just about 9 months; now that the birthing process is over, I'm looking at the rearing and nurturing aspects. I hope that you are not exactly the same person as you were, either; communication is always a two-way process, and books are no exception. I hope that you have found some truths in here, some seeds that may bear fruit; and especially that you have enjoyed reading it.

One thing that is important, which I may not have made obvious, is that I am working in this book with a specific viewpoint on myth. Myths are many-faceted, multi-layered, and there are many, many ways of looking at them and working with them. Bruno Bettelheim, for instance, in his work *The Uses of Enchantment* (Penguin) has much to say about the sociological and developmental functions of myth and fairy tale

144

in children (to say nothing of their function as gateways into the world of magic, imagination and creativity.) I haven't even touched on this area, and as Bettelheim's book is such a classic, I strongly recommend that you read it. (For a full list of relevant works, please refer to the Notes section. And if you only read one book from the many detailed, make it *Women Who Run With the Wolves* if you are a woman, or *Iron John* if you are a man.) Another thing that I should mention here is that I have placed great emphasis on myths as charts of the inner journey. They are; but they also have much to say about our outer lives, too. As you read them, read them as it were 'bi-focally', one eye on them as messages for the inner world, the other on them as guidelines for our outer lives with all their interpersonal complexities. The one approach does not preclude the other.

Finally to sum up the practicalities. By now, you should have:

- established an inner sanctuary for yourself, and created physical sacred space, and hopefully regular practice,
- some idea of the realms of Soul, Spirit and the nature of the Self,
- determined which is your dominant psychological type, and made a commitment to yourself to spend time nurturing your less-developed function,
- followed this up with the Four Directions exercise in Chapter 4, which is intended to explore this idea further,
- possibly made a Medicine Wheel,
- perhaps got an idea of what your 'power-animal' may be; specific instructions for this can be found in the various books on shamanism detailed in the Notes,
- found one of 'your' myths. If it is a positive/healing myth there is little you need to do with it. If, however, its message is largely negative (or you experience it as such) or tragic, you will have summed-up its message in a sentence, created a counter-statement or positive affirmation, and hopefully have started on the process of re-writing it/changing its ending, and finding a healing myth. You will also have 'told your story' in the process, and worked with your Lifeline on paper,
- learned to look at myths in a new way,
- taken a journey to the Healing Spring,
- and learned a little about your relationship to anima/animus, or the masculine and feminine within, via the quest for the Grail treasures.

If there are any of the above that you have not yet experienced, now is the time. In any case, it's worth taking a pen and
paper, or your journal – *now* – and spending half-an-hour
responding to the above points.

We are moving towards a new era. No one has been here
before, and what we make of it is up to us, each of us. We need
a new world order based on love, not power; we need male and
female side-by-side offering their unique and complementary
gifts. It is possible. Patriarchy has not worked; matriarchy is
not the answer. No doubt there is a term for the co-existence
and rule in love, equality and harmony of both sexes, but I
can't think of it. However, first the well-maidens still need to
be restored before the land can be made whole; we still have
much work to do in honouring the feminine before the new
order can be brought to birth. One important thing is for us all,
men and women, to search out the healing myths, especially
the myths that address feminine values, and in which self-
determining women win through. Other than for the purposes
of discovering where you are 'stuck', *don't* read myths where
the women lose out. Rapunzel, Cinderella, Gretal all go
through horrendous ordeals but win out. *The Little Match-Girl*
does not, unless you count dying and going to heaven as
winning through. Nor does *The Little Mermaid*.

Feinstein and Krippner in *Personal Mythology* quote Rollo
May as saying that we need three new categories of myth. One
is the 'green myth', which would depict our healthy relation
with nature; one is the feminist myth, which in its broadest
sense would recognize the talents and ensure the rights of all
people, and the third is the idea of 'planetism', which, political
boundaries transcended, would depict the world as 'global
village'. *You* can help make this difference. The 'critical mass'
theory maintains that there is a point at which sufficient
weight, sufficient number, can tip a balance. We are moving
towards this pivotal point. We don't know what the 'critical
mass' needed to effect this change is, but there is evidence that
it happens. You may be the Hundredth Monkey (and if this
term is new to you, I leave you with a mystery to investigate!
Suffice it to say that the Hundredth Monkey is the hypothetical
critical number that enables the species to make a quantum
leap in consciousness.)

And lastly, leave a little room for chaos in your life, room for the creative spark to breathe. And don't forget your star-fire nature. Nietzsche said: 'You have to have a chaos within you to give rise to a dancing star.'

Notes

EPIGRAPH

1. Joseph Campbell, *The Hero with a Thousand Faces*, Paladin, 1988.

INTRODUCTION AND AUTHOR'S NOTE

1. Lindsay Clarke, from a lecture at the Dartington Conference, 1992.
2. Matthew Fox, from a lecture at the Dartington Conference, 1993.
3. See also Robert Bly, *Iron John*, Element, 1990; and also his workshop tapes.

CHAPTER 1. CREATING SACRED SPACE

1. Robert Bly, *Iron John*.
2. T. S. Eliot, 'Burnt Norton', from the *Four Quartets* (*Collected Poems*, Faber, 1974).
3. Abraham Maslow, *The Farther Reaches of Human Nature*, Pelican, 1973.
4. John Davidson, *Subtle Energy*, C. W. Daniel, 1987.
5. Annie Dillard, *Pilgrim at Tinker Creek*, Picador, 1976.
6. Ibid.
7. Ibid.
8. Matthew Fox, from a lecture at the Dartington Conference, 1993.

CHAPTER 2. THE LIGHTED FIELD OF CONSCIOUSNESS

1. Mark Thurston, *Discovering Your Soul's Purpose*, Edgar Cayce Foundation, ARE Press, 1984.
2. John C Lilly, *The Centre of the Cyclone*, Paladin, 1973.
3. From the Foreword by William Booth in Robert Bly, *A Little Book on the Human Shadow*, Element, 1992.

4. T. Dethlefsen and R. Dahlke, *The Healing Power of Illness*, trans. Peter Lemesurier, Element, 1990.
5. Ibid.

CHAPTER 3. FIRE, AIR, WATER AND EARTH

1. Jean Shinoda Bolen, in the introduction to her book *Goddesses in Everywoman* (Harper Colophon, 1985), which has been an enormously helpful book to me personally, challenges this system of typology. I acknowledge her work as being equally valid, and any interested reader or anyone who feels that there are shortcomings in Jung's approach as I have described it, is referred to this book and its sequel, *Gods in Everyman*. As always, it is a question of 'and/ and' rather than 'either/or'. For the purposes of this book I feel that while Jung's approach to this categorization may not contain absolute truth, it does contain the wisdom of certain truths, and as such provides a clear model.
2. C. G. Jung, *Modern Man in Search of a Soul*, ARK, 1984, p. 105.
3. Ibid., p. 107.
4. Ibid., p. 107.
5. Much of this information comes from E. M. W. Tillyard's *The Elizabethan World Picture*, Penguin, 1963.
6. Quoted in Liz Greene, *Relating*, Aquarian, 1986.
7. Ngakpa Chogyam, *Rainbow of Liberated Energy*, Element, 1986.

CHAPTER 4. A SHAMANIC MAP OF THE WORLD

1. Matthew Fox, *Original Blessing*, Bear and Co., 1983.
2. Ohiyesa, from T. C. McLuhan, *Touch of the Earth*, Abacus, 1973.
3. Gabrielle Roth, *Maps to Ecstasy*, Mandala, 1990.
4. Michael Harner, *The Way of the Shaman*, Harper Collins, 1980.
5. Nicki Scully, *The Golden Cauldron: Shamanic Journeys on the Path of Wisdom*.
6. These extracts from her book are taken from an article in *Kindred Spirit* magazine, Summer 1993.
7. John Matthews, *The Celtic Shaman*, Element, 1991.
8. John Matthews, *The Song of Taliesin – Stories and Poems from the Books of Broceliande*, Aquarian, 1991.
9. Lynn V. Andrews, *Star Woman*, Warner Books, 1987.
10. Kenneth Meadows, *Earth Medicine*, Element, 1989.

CHAPTER 5. THE WORLD OF MYTH

1. In myth, the serpent/dragon often demands the sacrifice (payment) of youths and maidens – that is the giving-up of youthful folly – before it reveals its wisdom. If it is not acknowledged, it just devours the life-energy mercilessly.

CHAPTER 6. LIVING MYTHOLOGY

1. From the Foreword to Feinstein and Krippner, *Personal Mythology*, Mandala, 1989.
2. Ibid.
3. Feinstein and Krippner, *Personal Mythology*.
4. From Clarissa Pinkola Estes, *Women Who Run with the Wolves*, Rider, 1992.

PSYCHE AND EROS

1. The full text of this tale can be found in Apuleius, *The Golden Ass* translated by Robert Graves, Penguin Classics, 1950. See also Robert Johnson's *She*, Perennial Library, 1989.

CHAPTER 7. THE HEROIC QUEST

1. Marge Piercy, 'Circling', *Living in the Open*, Alfred A. Knopf Inc.
2. T. S. Eliot, 'Little Gidding', *Four Quartets*, Faber & Faber, 1974.
3. Joseph Campbell, *The Hero With a Thousand Faces* (also *Myths to Live By*, Bantam, 1972.)
4. Brian Patten, *Love Poems*, Unwin, 1984.
5. Jerome Peignot, *Les jeux de l'amour et du langage*, 10/18 – Union Generale D'Editions, 1974.
6. Lizzie Spring, 'In The Dark', *First Things*, Diamond Press.
7. Robert Johnson, *She*.
8. See also Jean Shinoda Bolen, *Goddesses in Everywoman*. Some of the information on the four tasks has come from this book.
9. Clarissa Pinkola Estes, *Women Who Run with the Wolves*.
10. Robert Johnson, *She*.

THE QUEST FOR THE HOLY GRAIL

1. John Matthews, *The Grail – Quest for the Eternal*, Thames and Hudson, 1989.

2. The Grail Maiden, Repanse de Schoye. My knowledge of mediaeval French is very scanty, and I cannot find a translation of her name anywhere. However it seems to me that it would be fitting if this translates as Reponse de Joie – Joyful Answer. I admit too that this may just be wishful thinking!
3. Blanchefleur, which means 'White Flower', is likely to be a synonym for Soul (as too sometimes is 'Dove'),

CHAPTER 8. TOWARDS WHOLENESS

1. William Blake, *The Marriage of Heaven and Hell*.
2. In *Myths and Legends of the Celtic Race*, Constable, 1985.
3. Emma Jung and Marie-Louise von Franz, *The Grail Legend*, trans. Andrea Dykes, Coventure, 1986.
4. Ibid., p. 260.
5. The symbols in this telling are Christianized versions of the four archetypal motifs of cup or cauldron; sword; spear, lance or wand; and plate, dish, coin or pentacle. The Paten or Dish is the plate on which the bread/host was served at the Last Supper, the Lance the spear of Longinus which pierced Christ's side at the Crucifixion, and the Grail the chalice that received his blood/ wine, and which some say was brought to Britain (Glastonbury) with Joseph of Arimathea. (Others have it that the Grail was delivered into the keeping of the Cathars – whether as a physical vessel or as Sacred Teachings is debated.)
    In some versions of the legend the Grail is a stone rather than a vessel, and has been identified with the Lapis of transformation of which the alchemists spoke.
6. See Robert Johnson, *The Psychology of Romantic Love*, Arkana, 1987. Also, for further illumination on Parsifal, his book *He*, Perennial Library, 1989.
7. Rainer Maria Rilke:

    . . . once the realization is accepted that, even between the closest human beings, infinite distances continue to exist, a wonderful living side-by-side can grow up, if they succeed in loving the distance between them which makes it possible for each to see the other whole an against a wide sky!

8. Wagner, *Parsifal*.
9. Emma Jung and Marie-Loiuse von Franz, *The Grail Legend*, p. 181.
10. Ibid., pp. 175, 183–4.

Appendix I

THE 'TREE' EXERCISE FOR GROUNDING

Stand upright, feet (preferably bare) slightly apart and firmly planted. Relax your body and breathe deeply into your lower abdomen three or four times. Now as you breathe draw the breath down through your body to your feet; see the breath helping to root your feet to the ground. Wriggle your toes and imagine that they are planted in rich moist loamy soil; your roots go down way way below the earth's crust, drawing nourishment and strength from the ground, holding you firm against storm and flood. Stay aware of your breath, and slowly start to lift your arms above your head, and gently open your hands, move your fingers; feel sunlight on your crown of leaves and branches, a soft breeze inviting you to dance. Allow yourself to sway lightly with the wind, all the time breathing deeply, keeping your feet rooted. From time to time a wingtip may brush your branches; squirrels may scurry around your feet. Imagine your highest branches drawing light down into them, sending it flowing through your body and into your rooted feet; a river of light connecting your head to your heart to your feet, a golden stream linking heaven and earth.

When you are ready, slowly lower your arms, wriggle your toes, open your eyes.

Appendix 2

A cassette-tape is available that contains two of the visualizations (the Sanctuary and the Healing Spring). For this and for details of Myth and the Inner Journey workshops please send sae to the following address:

Roselle Angwin
PO Box 17
Yelverton
Devon PL20 6YF

Glossary

Alchemy Ostensibly the art of transforming base metals into gold. Its inward parallel was the journey of the soul. On the inner plane its concern was the refinement and purification of one's being, and the reconciliation (through the Sacred Marriage) of opposites.

Anchorite A religious recluse, hermit.

Androgyne One who is both male and female, gender undifferentiated. The 'Divine Androgyne' is one who is beyond the dualism implied in the division of humans into male and female.

Anima The inner female component of a man's psyche.

Animus The inner male component of a woman's psyche.

Anthropocentric A view of the universe that is people-centred.

Archetype(s) 'The original pattern or model, prototype' (Chambers). Contents of the collective unconscious that manifest in universal images that have existed since the remotest times. Embodiments of particular forces/influences in universally occurring symbolic form.

Ariadne's thread Ariadne fell in love with Theseus who was to be sacrificed to the Minotaur, and gave him a ball of thread by which he was able to find his way back out of the labyrinth.

Artemis Greek moon-goddess associated with wild creatures, fertility (though she herself was chaste) and hunting. Protectress of young women.

Athena Greek goddess of wisdom and warfare. Patroness of heroic men.

Centred To be fully present in the here and now with your body, mind, emotions and spirituality in balance. A condition of being fully oneself.

Chakra From the Sanskrit meaning 'wheel' or 'disc'. Whirling power-centres in the subtle body that act as focal points receiving and transmitting subtle energy.

Collective unconscious Jung says that it is a deeper layer underpinning the personal unconscious that does not derive from personal experience or acquisition but is inborn. Of universal origin, its contents and modes of behaviour are more-or-less identical everywhere and in all individuals, though expression of them through the personal psyche may vary from age to age and culture to culture.

Consciousness Condition of being awake, aware and present. David V. Tansley says 'The union of spirit and matter manifests as consciousness.'

Dualism Belief-system based on the opposition of spirit and matter, good and evil, etc.

Earthing What a friend described as the process of firmly connecting your head to your feet and your feet to the ground. The earthing process, which may involve eating, drinking or an exercise such as the 'Tree' exercise in Appendix I, helps to ensure your safe return to everyday reality after inner journeying.

Ego The 'I' or everyday self, that which is conscious and thinks, to which is attached the personality.

Enantiodromia From Heraclitus, meaning 'to flow backwards'. Used by Jung in his typology work to describe the process by which, occasionally, an individual, often as a result of trauma, 'flips' psychologically from his/her normal 'superior' function into a person of the opposite type; for example, a sensation-function person might suddenly become an intuitive.

Energy 'The power projected by a vibratory force' (Kenneth Meadows).

Enlightenment A leap in consciousness when suddenly everything is seen in perfect clarity, exactly as it is. Often preceded by acute spiritual anguish and inner tension. It requires a giving up of trying to 'understand' intellectually, and a letting go, or rather a leaping, into the Void. Some traditions make use of catalysts such as intensive prayer, meditation, chanting, Zen koans, drumming, etc. Altered states of consciousness due to hallucinogens, and some peak experiences, can give moments of this kind of insight.

Eros Greek god of love. The principle that strives to unite the elements of the cosmos into harmony. Eros is involved in soul-making through erotic connections, imagination and creativity, and represents a passionate rather than a rational principle.

Existentialist Pertaining to questions/issues about the state of existence, meaning, the *raison d'être*. Also doctrine that denies objective universal values and holds that each person must create values for him/herself through action and the will-to-action, and through living each moment to the full.

Extrovert One whose main focus of attention is the external world.

Four Functions Described by Jung as being the fourfold aspects of perceiving, judging and evaluating experience through the intellect, emotions, intuition or sensation, corresponding respectively with air, water, fire and earth.

Gestalt A branch of psychology that assumes that 'human nature is organized into patterns or wholes, that it is experienced by the individual in these terms, and that it can only be understood as a function of the patterns or wholes of which it is made' (Fritz Perls).

Gods/Goddesses Higher beings; archetypes of divinity.

Grounding *See* **Earthing**.

Hallows The Grail Treasures, usually seen to be the Cup (or Grail), the Sword, the Spear and a shallow Dish, or (sometimes) Stone. These vary from account to account, and occasionally we hear of a fifth mysterious Treasure. The Four Hallows correspond to the elements/functions.

Humours Four fluids of the physical body – blood, phlegm, black bile, yellow bile – which were in mediaeval times supposed to determine temperament (that is, sanguine, phlegmatic, melancholic, choleric.) There is – you've guessed! – a correspondence with the elements.

Individuation The process of becoming whole, fully oneself; contacting one's essential nature and heeding the spirit. Involves some degree of initial separation from the collective and its values.

Introvert Someone whose main focus and attention is directed more towards their inner world than to the external, in contrast to the extrovert.

Karma Buddhist conception of the laws of cause and effect that determine the future condition of all sentient beings, releasing them from, or binding them to, the Wheel of this earthly life in future incarnations as a result of present-life actions.

Kundalini Great primary force that energizes all forms. In traditional Indian teachings it is seen in the human as a coiled serpent lying at the base of the spine. When the disciple is ready – sufficiently enlightened – kundalini power rises up the spine through the chakras.

Logos Classically means the 'Divine Word'. I have used it to mean the principle of order, reason, law, logic, objectivity, intellectually determined action – a force in opposition to Eros. This principle is embodied in the Apollo/Zeus archetype that has been the model for our patriarchal culture.

Mandala A circular artform with a spiritual focus painted in or for meditation. It symbolizes the Self and the Source, and also the totality of being. It is frequently eight-armed, often resembling a wheel. (Many spiritual/psychological traditions hold the number eight to be central to their practice.)

Mantra A sacred text or phrase used as an incantation or prayer and repeated.

Maya From the Sanskrit, meaning illusion.

Medicine Wheel A symbolic and meditative device used in American Indian teachings to focus the mind, obtain knowledge and facilitate entry into a different order of reality. Usually physical; often an impermanent creation of stones carefully placed, most often in groups of four or eight.

Mystical Involving a sacred or secret meaning visible to those who are spiritually enlightened. Concerned with Mystery teachings, communion with the Divine.

Numinous Pertaining to divinity.

Otherworld A more subtle dimension of being that nonetheless borders and overlaps our own experience of everyday reality. Time and space do not exist in this world, and it is populated by archetypal beings. Shamanic work involves entry into this dimension, usually in search of help, healing and guidance.

Palimpsest 'A manuscript in which old writing has been rubbed out to make room for new' (Chambers). I have used it as an image to describe how something can be subtly reinforced, changed or transformed by the addition of successive layers over the existing one(s).

Panentheis A term used by Matthew Fox to describe the belief that God is *in* everything (subtly distinct from **Pantheism**).

Pantheis The belief that everything is God, or that God is everything.

Peak experience Difficult to describe verbally. Loosely – an experience of supreme bliss, transcendent ecstasy, perfect harmony, etc. that temporarily takes us out of ourselves into a different way of being. Can be triggered by beauty, by nature, by music, by a sense of oneness with another or others, by falling in love, by sex, dancing, by the awareness that you have stumbled on a profound truth, for instance. We find it difficult to talk about in our culture as we no longer have a collectively valued vehicle or container for these experiences, which are similar to religious or mystical ecstasy.

Persona The outermost expression of the personality, the 'mask' that we all wear at the interface between oneself and the outer world.

Personal unconscious That layer of the mind of which we are not normally aware. Its contents are repressed material, memories, experiences, dreams, fantasies, acquired and learned patterns of thought and behaviour that may direct us and that may rise up spontaneously; normally a strong ego will control the contents of the unconscious world, to a greater or lesser extent, in daily living. If however the ego is weak, or there is much trauma, or the contents of the unconscious are repressed too severely or for too long, the unconscious may rebel and the ego may be overwhelmed, when a breakdown of some sort may occur. This realm is instinctual and irrational. For the purposes of this book the unconscious is seen to be feminine in tone, the realm of the Soul. I have also called it the Underworld as distinguished from the Upper world of Spirit (though classically the Underworld was seen to be the realm of the dead).

Projection A psychological process whereby our own unconscious material (often, though not necessarily, negative) is externalized and seen to be belonging to others, or to a significant other. The opposite happens in introjection.

Psyche With a capital 'P', in Greek mythology the young woman beloved of Eros; the personification of the Soul. With a small 'p' the soul, spirit or mind, or all three; the principle of emotional, mental and vital (but intangible) life, conscious or unconscious.

Psychosis Severe mental disorder where there is little contact with everyday reality.

Puer aeternus/Puella aeterna Literally 'eternal youth' – a term used by Jung and his followers to describe someone who, no matter what their age, remains the archetypal adolescent.

Self or **Higher Self** Used here to mean the unchanging essence of an individual, the divine spark, that which connects him or her to the Source. One's Centre. It is unaffected by the fluctuations of all aspects of egoic living. The Self focuses on the whole, and is concerned with the welfare of the collective rather than just the personal. It could also be called the Transpersonal Self.

Shadow Jung once defined the Shadow as the whole unconscious. Marie-Louise von Franz later defined it further as '. . . a mythological name for all that within me of which I cannot directly know'. We could also describe it as the repository of all those parts of ourselves which we, our parents or our community don't like, which we therefore repress.

Shaman One who 'walks between the worlds' in order to gain insight, wisdom or healing for himself or another. Someone who is adept at entering non-ordinary reality. To a shaman, there is life in everything and all things are sacred.

Shape-shifting Involves an exchange of energy with archetypal beings, usually animals, in order to facilitate a shaman in 'walking between the worlds'. He or she may appear as, and will perceive the world as, this other being. Usually in shamanic cultures this transformation occurs after much ritual preparation, including meditation, drumming, dance, solitude, fasting or the use of hallucinogenic drugs. The transformation lends the participant the power of the animal concerned.

Soul There are many ways of looking at the soul, as with the spirit. I have used Soul in this book fairly specifically. I have portrayed it as feminine in nature, concerned with connections and the collective, erotic, instinctual and undifferentiated. Its realm is the unconscious world and it is our personal portion of the collective unconscious and World-Soul. It offers us insight in the form of dreams and fantasies. While the Spirit provides the spark, the Soul provides the fuel for creativity.

Spirit I have used Spirit to mean the 'masculine' impulse upwards, belonging to the light realm of the superconscious, concerned with inspiration, individuation, differentiation. Its energy is 'spiritual' rather than erotic. Needless to say, Soul and Spirit need each other, and where the two meet is Mind, Imagination.

Styx The River that borders Hades, across which the souls of the dead are ferried.

Superconscious For the purposes of this book this is the Upperworld transcendent realm of Spirit, masculine, fiery and source of intuitive and 'higher' spiritual impulses, the 'will-to-good'.

Symbol An archetypal image that carries a 'charge' of energy and is a link between different orders of reality, different states of consciousness. Though it may be recognized immediately intuitively it cannot be so easily understood intellectually.

Synchronicity Simultaneously occurring events that are not linked causally or necessarily spatially.

Talisman A symbolic and protecting object, often used for inner journeying. Can represent the Self, or a less-conscious part of the person concerned.

Totem In Medicine Wheel teachings, a symbolic representation, usually of a living entity, which acts as a link between different levels of existence/reality.

Transcendence 'Rising above'. '. . . refers to the very highest and most inclusive or holistic levels of consciousness' (Maslow).

Transpersonal 'Beyond the personal' – concerned with the spiritual and collective dimensions of the psyche, and the well-being of the collective. The realm of the Self.

Tuatha de Danaan The original mythical invaders and colonizers of Ireland, literally 'descendants of the god whose mother was Dana'.

The Wasteland A condition of utmost desolation, sterility and barrenness, applied to the spiritual plane as well as the physical, resulting from violent destructiveness, ignorance, carelessness and imbalance. Originally mentioned in the Grail legends as a reflection of the Fisher King's condition (and vice versa). The subject of a famous poem of the same name by T. S. Eliot.

Yang The masculine principle in oriental thought, seen as active, outgoing and light.

Yin The complementary feminine principle, seen as still, receptive and dark.

Zeitgeist Literally, 'the spirit of the time'.

Index

Lilly, John C. xv, 24
love, romantic 133–5

Maslow, Abraham 6
Matthews, John 59, 60, 80
May, Rollo 146
Mead, Margaret xvii
Meadows, Kenneth 5, 62–3
Medicine Wheel 14, 60–1, 62–4,
    111, 145
meditation 14, 16–17
monomyth 103–6
Myers–Briggs system 38
myths, animals in 76–8
    as collective dreams 28, 70
    as metaphors xviii–xxii, 82
    as vehicles for insight 69
    heroic and tragic 85–6
    human figures in 73–6
    personal xii–xiii, 80–3, 85,
        86–90

Native American teachings 57,
    59, 60–4
nature 54–6, 58

Otherworld 6, 27–8, 59, 72, 75,
    77, 118, 128, 132, 137, 140

Parsifal *see* Perceval
Patten, Brian 106
Peignot, Jerome 107
Perceval (Parsifal) 74, 105, 112,
    121–6, 128–30, 132, 135–41
Peredur 121, 128, 131, 136
place, power of 9–11
power-animals 59, 72, 73, 112
Prather, Hugh 21
Psyche 95–102, 105, 110, 111–16,
    117–18
psyche 26–8, 71–2

rhythm, natural 3–4, 32
ritual 13–15

Rolleston, T. W. 129
Roth, Gabrielle 57

Scully, Nicki 58
Self xv–xvi, 22, 23–6, 63, 64, 65,
    75, 104, 108–9, 127, 129, 137,
    141, 145
sensation 34–5, 36, 37, 40–1, 51,
    65
senses 11–12
Shadow 29–32, 130
shamans 56–60
shape-shifting 59–60, 70–1, 112
Singer, June 80
Smith, J. D. 41
Somers, Barbara 24–5
Soul 111, 127, 145
superconscious 26, 71, 129
symbols 8, 14, 70, 71–2, 73–9,
    103, 110, 113–14, 121, 127–8,
    138, 141

Taliesin 60
Tarot 41, 42, 43, 44, 74
tests 112–16
thinking 34, 36, 37, 42, 52
Thurston, Mark 23, 38
Tristan 106, 107
Tuatha de Danaan 41, 42, 43,
    44

unconscious 26, 71, 87, 107,
    110–111, 129, 131
Underworld 100–1, 111, 116–18,
    140

visualization xxiv, 14–15, 17–19

water 39, 40, 41–2, 44, 52, 61, 66,
    115–16
wholeness xi, 104, 108, 130, 132
Wolfram von Eschenbach 121,
    129, 141
wounding 83–5, 130